Carry On Films

Other books in this series by the same author

Agatha Christie
Doctor Who
Sherlock Holmes

Carry On Films

Mark Campbell

www.pocketessentials.com

This edition published in 2005 by Pocket Essentials
P.O.Box 394, Harpenden, Herts, AL5 1XJ

Distributed in the USA by Trafalgar Square Publishing, P.O. Box 257, Howe Hill
Road, North Pomfret, Vermont 05053
http:// www.pocketessentials.com

A CIP catalogue record for this book is available from the British Library.

ISBN 1 904048 42 0

2 4 6 8 10 9 7 5 3 1

Typeset by Avocet Typeset, Chilton, Aylesbury, Bucks
Printed and bound in Great Britain by Cox & Wyman, Reading, Berks

For Simon

Acknowledgements

Special thanks to Christine, Linda and the greatly missed Martina at the Slade Library, Plumstead, for their invaluable help in obtaining books and videos; to Iain Jarvis and Ian Long for plugging the gaps; to Anne and Andreas Rudloff for translating German over the 'phone; to Andy Slater for giving me his PC and navigating me through south-east London in the rush hour; to Jason Tomes for 'Name That Tune'; to David Benson for good advice; to Andy Davidson at Carry On Line for his help and support; to Steve Holland for not cracking the whip; to my friends at Woolwich Community Church for their support (especially Pete and Richard); to my wife Mary for proof-reading and putting up with me while I sat at home watching *Carry On* films ('Of course it's work!'); to my children Ben and Emily for their pertinent observations ('*Carry On Don't Lose Your Head* sounds weird'); and last but not least to Jesus Christ for his continued grace and mercy.

Contents

CONTENTS

Infamy, Infamy…

You know the story – a classic British film series that began in the 1950s, reached its heights in the 1960s and tailed off in quality until it ceased production in the late 1970s; a small, repertory cast of actors and actresses appearing countless times in similar roles; ludicrous scenarios and hilarious dialogue; plenty of heaving bosoms and scantily-clad blondes… but enough of Hammer horror films, let's talk about the *Carry Ons*.

Britain's three main film exports – Hammer, *Carry On* and James Bond – all have one thing in common. Regardless of whether you think they're good or bad, they all display a constancy of tone and technique that marks them out as being cast from the same mould. Blindfolded, you'd know you were watching a Hammer film by the portentous music, hoof-beat sound effects and stilted dialogue. Or a James Bond by the operatic score and dry delivery of unlikely lines. The same goes for *Carry On* films. Each and every one of them has the same *Tom And Jerry*-style 'comedy' soundtrack, the same arch delivery of pointed innuendo, the same stereotyped characters. As a friend once said to me, '*Carry On* films are so *reassuring*.' And he's right – even the bad ones can buoy you up, in a resigned, 'I don't believe I'm watching this rubbish, but what the heck, I can't be bothered to turn over' kind of way. You stop, sit back a little, ponder idly to yourself which *Carry On* it might be, before either giving in and watching it, or (if you're made of sterner stuff) switching to reruns of *Frasier*. The *Carry Ons* exhibit a primitive magnetism, drawing you into their own little world of schoolboy smut and silly pratfalls in the same way that a snake hypnotises a mouse. Once captured, it's very diffi- cult to escape. 'Just five more minutes,' you say to yourself, trying not to think of that huge pile of dirty crockery waiting to be washed. But then you realise you know what's going to happen next ('Oh, I remember this,' you mutter), and you give it a further five minutes. And another five. The fact that most *Carry Ons* are watched again and again over the years – the scenes burnt into the brain like a channel ident on a plasma screen – adds to their cosy, feel-good appeal. We're virtually born with all the jokes from *Carry On Cleo* hardwired into our DNA. The films go beyond simple cinematic entertainments and into the very fabric of our society. They're as deep-rooted as our national identity, as vital as the air we breathe. They're icons of pop culture, like *The Magic Roundabout* or The Beatles. They define who we are.

Alternatively, they're just 31 efficiently made light comedies of a rather old-fashioned kind starring a team of actors and actresses who were very good at what they did but are now mostly all dead. We may laugh at them but let's be clear about one thing – it's not because we find them funny. Our laughter is more hard-edged; the sort of sneering laugh that we might bestow on an old *Benny Hill Show* perhaps, as if to say, 'Is that what they called funny in those days? Oh dear!' To misquote a 1990s compilation series, we're not really laughing *with* the *Carry Ons*, we're laughing *at* them. They're relics of the past, museum pieces seen through rose-tinted spectacles in which fat people are funny, nurses strip to their undies and frustrated husbands drool over women with unfeasibly large breasts. If there's a banana skin, someone will slip on it. If there's a foreigner, he'll be a villain or a fool. Characters are called Tingle and Bigger and Nookey. The action takes place on a 1950s housing estate in Slough. I mean, it's all so *passé*. How can anyone think they're any good? More pertinently, how can anyone find them funny anymore?

A few years ago a noted academic voted *Carry On... Up the Khyber* his favourite film – leading to a furore in the media and a clutch of *Daily Mail*-type editorials about falling standards in further education. But the reason this chap chose *Khyber* was that it made him laugh, simple as that. He didn't bother to consider whether it was a 'good' film (whatever that means), just whether it did its job. And it did – perfectly. Let's face it, *Up the Khyber* is a hundred times funnier than *Citizen Kane* or *Raging Bull*. There was also a class element to the story – it is generally assumed that the *Carry On* films were designed (unconsciously I think) to appeal to a working-class audience – the 'masses' who liked vulgar humour and toilet jokes. Unlike the middle and upper classes, you see, who spend their time chuckling politely over the refined wit of Wodehouse and Belloc. Of course, this compartmentalising of the classes is always a dangerous notion, and with the *Carry On* films it's clear that they were (and still are) enjoyed by people of all classes, ages and social backgrounds. 'If something's funny, it's funny no matter what school you were bullied at,' Woody Allen notably didn't say. I reckon the Queen herself enjoys a crafty peep at *Carry On Henry* when she's not being called upon to plant a tree or open a new civic centre. And Tony Blair's favourite is surely *Carry On Regardless*. (Little bit of politics, as Ben Elton might say.)

What I'm trying to say in my roundabout way is that the *Carry On* films are universally derided but universally loved. We've all watched them, even though deep down inside we know there's something more important we should be getting on with. Produced by one man (Peter Rogers), directed by another (Gerald Thomas) and featuring an almost unchanging team of character actors, the *Carry On*s typify the idiom, 'If you're going to do it, do it well.' Even if it's only an innuendo-filled farce filmed on the cheap (Kenneth Williams was never paid more than £5,000 per film) over four weeks in a draughty Pinewood studio, it makes no difference – do it well, or don't do it at all. And in my opinion, the *Carry On* series did do it well, with a few notable exceptions.

For what it's worth, my formula for the perfect *Carry On* would be as follows – no Barbara Windsor, narration by Raymond Allen, several men in drag, a 'c' sound in the title (no, seriously), a historical setting and no speeded-up sequences or stock footage. Alas, no film quite has them all, but of the many that come close, I offer *Cabby*, *Cleo*, *Cowboy*, *Screaming!*, *Don't Lose Your Head*, *Up the Khyber*, *Henry* and *Girls*. (I throw this last one in as the exception that proves the rule.)

Lastly, you've probably noticed that this book is only available in a handy, pocket-sized edition. Bearing this in mind I have taken the decision not to fill it with boring facts and figures. There are other writers far more capable of that than me. The film section – the bulk of this guide, naturally – thus consists of straightforward reviews rather than in-depth histories about how they were made and what socio-political ideology they represented. Sorry if that's your bag, but I feel you can kill comedy by over-analysing it, and that's never truer than with the *Carry On* films. So I have attempted to judge them on one criterion alone: are they funny?

And they are. You know they are…

Carry On Quizzing

Call yourself a true *Carry On* fan? Here is a selection of fiendishly cunning questions about the film series to frustrate and bemuse you. So get your thinking caps on and remember – no prizes, it's just for fun.

1) First lines – but from which film?
1) 'Ooh, how am I going to get all this lot in?'
2) 'I wonder what they wanted?'
3) 'Congratulations!'
4) 'Yes, speaking.'
5) 'Come in!'
6) 'Oh come on, what's keeping her?'
7) 'And you men have been especially chosen for one task.'
8) 'Well, bye-bye old lad, and thanks for an absolutely smashing weekend.'

2) Who said what, and in which film?
1) 'Gentlemen, have I your agreement for a policy of unremitting quasi-Teutonic organisational perfectionism?'
2) 'Now look, you've got to face up to it. You're an obsessional with visual complications.'
3) 'By Jove, a simian amorist with a paralysed conscience.'
4) 'It came off in my hand!'

5) 'Oh, I beseech you from my bowels!'
6) 'We have ways of making you talk!'
7) 'Oh, my head is broken!'
8) 'Oh, an epigram – oh I say, sir.'
9) 'I'm really engaged to a very well-known butcher in Wolverhampton.'

3) In which films were these characters mentioned?
1) Fanny Fusspot
2) Aunt Lill
3) Lucy Nation
4) Farmer Giles
5) Beau Legs

4) Which films featured the following on-screen books?
1) 'Wooing to Win'
2) 'Fu-Kung Sex'
3) 'Ye Joyes of Ye Marriage Bed'
4) 'Articles of War'
5) 'The Angel Behind the Cosh'
6) 'They Do It for Fun'
7) 'Metamorphosis: A Study of the Sex Change in Man'
8) 'The Wit to Woo'
9) 'A Belle Parisienne'
10) 'Wakefield's Practical Surgery'
11) 'How to Avoid Sea Serpents'

Biographies

What follows are potted résumés of the key actors and technical personnel involved in the *Carry On* series. With regard to television series, dates in parenthesis refer to the entire run of the show in question.

Bernard Bresslaw *Actor* (25 February 1934 – 11 June 1993)
Bresslaw's comedy career began with the radio series *Educating Archie* (1958–59). He also worked on the Granada sitcom *The Army Game* (1957–61) alongside *Carry On* regular Charles Hawtrey, as well as its 1957 cinema spin-off, *I Only Arsked!*. Other television appearances included *The Bernard Bresslaw Show* (1958–59), *Bresslaw And Friends* (1961) and *Doctor Who* (as an Ice Warrior, 1967). His hulking presence made him the perfect gormless giant in the *Carry On* series, and he notched up 14 appearances, beginning with *Cowboy* (1965). In later life he found critical acclaim in serious roles.

Peter Butterworth *Actor* (4 February 1919 – 17 January 1979)
Butterworth met future *Carry On* scribe Talbot Rothwell in a German POW camp in the Second World War, where Rothwell persuaded him to perform in a camp concert in

order to distract attention away from an escape attempt. Butterworth married comedienne Janet Brown and appeared in many films and television shows, often as the bumbling stooge. His 16 *Carry On* films cover the rich period from *Cowboy* (1965) to *Emmannuelle* (1978).

Kenneth Connor *Actor* (6 June 1916 – 28 November 1993)
Connor made a name for himself in radio shows such as *Ray's A Laugh* (1949–61), starring music hall comedian and musician Ted Ray. In the *Carry On* series, he played shy, nervous romantic leads, beginning with *Sergeant* (1958), until this role was usurped by Jim Dale. After a gap of some years he returned to play character roles nearer his own age. As well as his 17 *Carry On* films, he guest-starred in *'Allo 'Allo!* (1982–92), *Hi-de-Hi!* (1980–88), *Blackadder the Third* (1987) and *Rentaghost* (1976–84).

Bernard Cribbins *Actor* (29 December 1928)
Lancashire-born Cribbins enjoyed a wide variety of film roles, from a policeman in *Daleks' Invasion Earth 2150 A.D.* (1966) to a stationmaster in *The Railway Children* (1970). He starred in three *Carry On* films and was responsible for the 1960s novelty songs *Right Said Fred* and *Hole in the Ground*. On television, he appeared in the second series of the sketch show *Get the Drift* (1971–76) and the Granada sitcom *Langley Bottom* (1986); he also memorably voiced the original series of *The Wombles* (1973).

Jim Dale *Actor* (15 August 1935)
Born James Smith, Dale trained as a dancer and singer, first coming to the public's attention on the BBC's pop music show *Six-Five Special* (1957–58). A successful, if

short-lived, career as a pop singer saw him reach no.2 in the charts with a song called *Be My Girl* in 1957. *Cabby* was the first of his 11 *Carry On* appearances, mostly as a clumsy romantic lead, but it was not until the final entry in the series, *Columbus* (1992), that he received top billing. He emigrated to America in the 1970s and, always keen to do his own stunts, took the title role in the original Broadway production of the circus musical *Barnum*.

Jack Douglas *Actor* (26 April 1927)
Born Jack Roberton, producing pantomimes at an early age gave Douglas a taste for comedy and he appeared in eight of the later *Carry Ons*, normally in the guise of fidgeting, arm-waving alter ego Alf Ippititimus. Television shows included sitcoms *Dave's Kingdom* (1964), *Not on Your Nellie* (1974–75) and *Cuffy* (1983).
A Twitch in Time by Sue Benwell & Jack Douglas, 2002

Derek Francis *Actor* (7 November 1923 – 27 March 1984)
Stout character actor, normally cast in pompous roles. He appeared in six *Carry Ons*, beginning with *Carry On Doctor* in 1967. Other films included Hammer smuggling yarn *Captain Clegg* (1962) and medieval comedy *Jabberwocky* (1977). On television he starred with Derek Nimmo in the last two series of *Oh Brother!* (1968–70), while guest appearances included *Doctor Who* (1963–present) and *Man in a Suitcase* (1967).

Liz Fraser *Actress* (14 August 1933)
Blonde Cockney comedienne. She played opposite Peter Sellers in *I'm All Right, Jack* (1959) and appeared in three early *Carry Ons*, beginning with *Regardless* (1961), before returning to the series over a decade later with *Behind*

(1975). A semi-regular in *Hancock's Half-Hour* (1956–60), she also popped up with Robin Asquith in two *Confessions* sex comedies: *Driving Instructor* (1976) and *Holiday Camp* (1977).

Peter Gilmore *Actor* (25 August 1931)
Tall, rugged and gruff-voiced, Gilmore appeared in 11 *Carry On* films, often playing heavies. On television he became famous as the star of the BBC seafaring series *The Onedin Line* (1971–1980). Notable film appearances included *The Great St Trinian's Train Robbery* (1966), *The Abominable Dr Phibes* (1971) and *Warlords of Atlantis* (1978), while in 1984 he appeared with this author in the radio drama *Early Unions and the Tolpuddle Martyrs*. The same year he made his one and only appearance in *Doctor Who* (1963–present).

Charles Hawtrey *Actor* (30 November 1914 – 27 October 1988)
Born George Frederick Joffre Hartree, the rake-thin Hawtrey enjoyed a prolific career in radio, theatre and films. He appeared as an unfeasibly old schoolboy in several Will Hay film farces in the late 1930s and early 1940s, and a role in the sitcom *The Army Game* (1957–61) led to a similar part in the first *Carry On* film, *Sergeant* (1958). He went on to star in 23 *Carry Ons*, but after long-standing wrangles over screen billing and an ongoing alcohol problem, producer Peter Rogers severed his connection after *Abroad* in 1972. Hawtrey subsequently retired to a cottage in Deal where he became an alcoholic recluse. He died after refusing an operation to amputate his legs.
Charles Hawtrey 1914–1988 – The Man Who Was Private Widdle by Roger Lewis, 2001

Julian Holloway *Actor* (24 June 1944)
The son of character actor and music-hall entertainer
Stanley Holloway, Julian made eight *Carry On* appear-
ances, usually in supporting roles. Other films included
Amicus horror flick *Scream and Scream Again* (1969) and
sitcom spin-off *Porridge* (1979). On television he appeared
in the PG Wodehouse series *Ukridge* (1968), the sitcom
Keep It in the Family (1980–83) and, in 1989, the last
regular *Doctor Who* story before its revival in 2005.
Through a brief relationship with actress and novelist
Tessa Dahl, he is the father of Sophie Dahl, the fashion
model and granddaughter of children's author Roald
Dahl.

Frankie Howerd *Actor* (6 March 1917 – 19 April 1992)
Born Francis Alick Howard, Howerd's stammer at first
proved a stumbling block to his showbusiness dreams,
although it later became integral to his stand-up routine.
In a television career spanning many sitcoms, he achieved
most recognition as Lurcio in *Up Pompeii!* (1970), written
mainly by *Carry On* scriptwriter Talbot Rothwell. His two
Carry On appearances – *Doctor* and *Up the Jungle* – came
at a high point in his career. He was awarded an OBE in
1977.
On the Way I Lost It – An Autobiography by Frankie
Howerd, 1976
Titter Ye Not! – The Life of Frankie Howerd by William Hall,
1992
Frankie Howerd – The Illustrated Biography by Mick
Middles, 2000
The Complete Frankie Howerd by Robert Ross, 2001
Frankie Howerd: Stand Up Comic by Graham McCann,
2004

Norman Hudis *Writer* (27 July 1922)
Trained as a newspaper reporter, Hudis teamed up with
Carry On producer Peter Rogers for Tommy Steele's 1957
biopic *Rock Around the World*. This led to him turning RF
Delderfield's novel *The Bull Boys* into *Carry On Sergeant*
(1958). Five further *Carry On*s followed, all with the same
premise. He moved to America in the 1960s where he
wrote for *The Man From U.N.C.L.E.* (1964–68) and
Hawaii Five-O (1968–80) amongst others.

Hattie Jacques *Actress* (7 February 1924 – 7 October
1980)
This outsize comedienne was a regular in the radio series
ITMA (1939–49) and *Hancock's Half-Hour* (1954–59), and
became a popular member of the *Carry On* team,
notching up 14 appearances. Her association with Eric
Sykes led to two popular BBC sitcoms, *Sykes and A...*
(1960–65) and its colour revival *Sykes* (1972–79), in
which she played his sister. For a time she was married to
actor John Le Mesurier, of *Dad's Army* fame.

Sid James *Actor* (8 May 1913 – 26 April 1976)
Born Sidney Joel Cohen in Johannesburg, South Africa,
Sid James trained briefly as an electrician before running
a hairdressing salon. He soon got interested in acting, and
appeared on stage in Johannesburg in *Double Error* by Lee
Thompson. During the Second World War he entertained
troops in Africa, emigrating to England on Christmas Day
1946. He made a name for himself as a heavy in gangster
films – he appeared as Lackery in *The Lavender Hill Mob*
(1951) – as well as joining future *Carry On* stars Kenneth
Williams and Hattie Jacques in the radio series *Hancock's
Half-Hour* (1954–59). Producer Peter Rogers used him to
replace Ted Ray in *Carry On Cabby* (1963), and the griz-

zled-looking actor went on to appear in a further 18 *Carry On* films. He also appeared in sitcoms such as *Citizen James* (1960–62), *George and the Dragon* (1966–68) and *Bless This House* (1971–76). A notorious womaniser and gambler, he had a string of affairs, most famously with co-star Barbara Windsor.

Sid James by Cliff Goodwin, 1995
The Complete Sid James by Robert Ross, 2000

Dilys Laye *Actress* (11 March 1934)
The petite, perky brunette appeared in four *Carry Ons*, starting with the first colour offering, *Cruising* (1962). Other films included *Blue Murder at St Trinian's* (1957) and *Petticoat Pirates* (1961). On television she guest-starred in *Campion* (1989–90) and was seen in the soap operas *EastEnders* (1984–present) and *Coronation Street* (1960–present).

Valerie Leon *Actress* (12 November 1945)
The face of 1970s Hai Karate adverts, this busty brunette made memorably sexy appearances in six *Carry On* films. Her filmwork included *The Italian Job* (1969), *Blood from the Mummy's Tomb* (1971) – playing a dual role as Egyptian princess and explorer's daughter – and *No Sex Please, We're British* (1973). She also played opposite two James Bonds: Roger Moore in *The Spy Who Loved Me* (1977) and Sean Connery in *Never Say Never Again* (1983).

Bruce Montgomery *Composer* (2 October 1921 – 15 September 1978)
Born in Chesterham Bois, Buckinghamshire, Montgomery studied at St John's College, Oxford where he was organist and choirmaster in the chapel. A close friend of Philip Larkin and Kingsley Amis, from 1944 to 1953 he

wrote mystery novels under the pen name of Edmund Crispin, featuring literary critic Professor Gervase Fen. By the late 1950s he was working almost entirely for the big screen, composing scores for such films as *The Kidnappers* (1953) and *The Truth about Women* (1957). He wrote the music for the first six black and white *Carry On*s, thus providing the familiar opening tune that has become synonymous with the series. His career later declined due to alcoholism.

Margaret Nolan *Actress* (1 August 1943)
Nolan started out as a glamour model (under the name Vickie Kennedy), before making arguably her most famous appearance as Dink in *Goldfinger* (1964). This was followed by *Carry On Cowboy*, the first of six *Carry On* appearances in which her voluptuous figure was always to the fore. She could also be seen in *The Great St Trinian's Train Robbery* (1966) and *Witchfinder General* (1968). Television work included all five series of Spike Milligan's seminal Q (1969–1980) and a 1972 episode of *Steptoe and Son* (1962–1974).

Jon Pertwee *Actor* (7 July 1919 – 20 May 1996)
Born John Devon Roland Pertwee, this inventive comic character actor, son of playwright Roland and father of actor Sean, was probably most famous in the early 1970s as the third *Doctor Who* (1963–present) and later as *Worzel Gummidge* (1979–87). During a long showbusiness career he appeared in innumerable films and television programmes and was a mainstay of popular radio show *The Navy Lark* (1959–77). He made larger-than-life appearances in four *Carry On*s, usually under heavy make-up.
Moon Boots and Dinner Suits by Jon Pertwee, 1984
I Am the Doctor by Jon Pertwee and David J Howe, 1996

Leslie Phillips *Actor* (20 April 1924)
This London-born light comedian often played suave
womanisers in films of the 1950s and 1960s. As well as
featuring in four *Carry On* films, beginning with *Nurse*
(1959), he was the star of the rival *Doctor* series and a
popular member of the BBC radio show *The Navy Lark*
(1959–77). He received an OBE in 1998 and currently
provides the voice of the Sorting Hat from the *Harry
Potter* films.

Eric Rogers *Composer* (25 September 1921 – 8 April 1981)
A church organist at the age of 13, Rogers composed
many comedy film scores in the 1960s and 1970s, as well
as transcribing Lionel Bart's notes for the hit musical
Oliver!. He took over from Bruce Montgomery on *Carry
On Cabby* (1963), building on the previous composer's
solid groundwork and going on to provide – in his 22
*Carry On*s – the distinctively confident and jaunty style of
music forever associated with the series.

Peter Rogers *Producer* (20 February 1914)
Born in Rochester, Kent, Rogers began his film career
writing religious scripts for Lord J Arthur Rank, then
worked as a scriptwriter for Gainsborough Pictures, later
producing children's films and adult thrillers. Creator and
driving force of the whole *Carry On* concept, he acted as
producer on all 31 films, although he was relegated to
Executive Producer on *Columbus* (1992). He was married
to the late Betty Box, producer of the *Doctor* series starring Dirk Bogarde, and, at the age of 91, he is currently
masterminding the proposed new *Carry On London* film
as well as working on his seventh novel.
Mr Carry On – The Life and Work of Peter Rogers by Morris
Bright and Robert Ross, 2001

Talbot Rothwell *Writer* (12 November 1916 – 28 February 1981)

Born in Bromley, Kent, Rothwell had a succession of jobs before settling as a writer. He wrote for the Crazy Gang and had several West End stage comedies under his belt when film producer Peter Rogers asked him to rewrite the script of *Call Me a Cab* – it swiftly became *Carry On Cabby* (1963), and Rothwell stayed with the series for the next 20 films. His bawdy humour and outrageous innuendo became a trademark of the series.

Patsy Rowlands *Actress* (19 January 1934 – 22 January 2005)

After a convent education, Rowlands joined the Little Players Theatre, like Hattie Jacques before her, and appeared in various films and TV series, including *Bless This House* (1971–76) with Sid James. In her nine *Carry On* films, she was unfairly pigeonholed as dowdy housewives or secretaries, often with an undercurrent of sexual frustration.

Terry Scott *Actor* (4 May 1927 – 26 July 1994)

Born John Owen Scott, this plump comic was known for his trouser-dropping stage farces and ongoing television appearances, including *Great Scott – It's Maynard!* (1955–56, with Bill Maynard) and *Hugh and I* (1962–68, with Hugh Lloyd). His most enduring sitcom began life as *Happy Ever After* (1974–78) and transmogrified into *Terry and June* (1979–1987), in which he shared the limelight with fellow *Carry On* star June Whitfield. He appeared in seven *Carry On* films, usually characterised as an overgrown schoolboy with a strong libido.

Joan Sims *Actress* (9 May 1930 – 28 June 2001)
Born Irene Joan Marion Sims, this multi-talented character actress holds the record for the greatest number of appearances by a female in the *Carry On* films – 24 in total. After leaving RADA at 19, a cameo appearance in *Doctor in the House* (1954) brought her to the attention of *Carry On* producer Peter Rogers (the *Doctor* series was produced by his wife, Betty Box). She appeared in the second *Carry On* film, *Nurse* (1959), and enjoyed an unbroken run from *Cleo* (1964) to *Emmannuelle* (1978). After the series finished, she made appearances in the BBC sitcoms *On the Up* (1990–92) and *As Time Goes By* (1992–2002).
High Spirits by Joan Sims, 2000

Gerald Thomas *Director* (10 December 1920 – 9 November 1993)
Born in Hull, Yorkshire, Thomas studied to become a doctor before entering the film industry in 1946, working as an assistant editor on such films as *The October Man* (1947) and Laurence Olivier's *Hamlet* (1948). A stickler for efficiency and speed (second takes were a rarity for him), he directed every *Carry On* film with military precision, often finishing ahead of schedule and always within budget.

June Whitfield *Actress* (11 November 1925)
This prolific comedienne achieved fame in 1953 playing Eth in the long-running radio series *Take It From Here* (1948–60). This led to many television appearances, including *The Tony Hancock Show* (1956–57), *Beggar My Neighbour* (1966–68) and, most famously, *Happy Ever After* (1974–78) and *Terry And June* (1979–1987), in which she co-starred with Terry Scott. Her most recent roles include

25

Jennifer Saunders' mother in *Absolutely Fabulous* (1992–present) and Miss Marple in BBC radio adaptations of various Agatha Christie stories. She appeared in four *Carry On* films, beginning with *Nurse* in 1959.

And June Whitfield by June Whitfield, 2000

Kenneth Williams *Actor* (22 February 1926 – 15 April 1988)

After finding fame as the Dauphin in George Bernard Shaw's *Saint Joan*, the nostril-flaring actor appeared on radio in *Hancock's Half-Hour* (1954–59), *Beyond Our Ken* (1958–64) and *Round the Horne* (1965–69), while at the same time starring in the burgeoning *Carry On* film series. He appeared in 26 *Carry On*s – although he denigrated them in his diaries – as well as such television programmes as *International Cabaret* (1966–68, 1974), in which he was the compère, and the children's storytelling series *Jackanory* (1965–96). He also provided voices for the 1981 BBC animated series *Willo the Wisp*. He was a mainstay of the long-running radio panel game *Just A Minute* (1967–present) and in later years found a comfortable niche as a chat show guest. He lived alone all his life, but had a wide circle of friends and was an enthusiastic diarist and letter writer.

Just Williams by Kenneth Williams, 1985

The Kenneth Williams Diaries edited by Russell Davies, 1993

The Kenneth Williams Letters edited by Russell Davies, 1994

The Complete Acid Drops by Kenneth Williams, 1999

Stop Messin' About: The Life of Kenneth Williams by Cliff Goodwin, 2005

Barbara Windsor *Actress* (6 August 1937)
The cheeky Cockney blonde actress was borne Barbara-
Ann Deeks, an only child, in Shoreditch, London. Her
first love was the theatre and she had a string of major
musical roles to her name, including Rosie in Lionel Bart's
1959 stage show *Fings Ain't What They Used To Be*. Her
first film was *The Belles of St Trinian's* (1954), also starring
Sid James and Joan Sims. Her first *Carry On* film was
1964's *Spying*, but she didn't appear again until *Carry On
Camping* (1969), eight films later. In all, she totalled ten
appearances. In the 1990s she became famous for playing
Queen Vic owner Peggy Mitchell in the BBC soap opera
EastEnders (1984–present).
Barbara – The Laughter and Tears of a Cockney Sparrow by
Barbara Windsor, 1990
All of Me – My Extraordinary Life by Barbara Windsor
(with Robin McGibbon), 2000

'Weigh Anchor!' (1958–1963)

Notes on the format:

Cast: Principal players, supporting artists and as many walk-on parts as is known

Crew: All credited behind-the-scenes people

DVD: R2 only unless otherwise stated; (SE) denotes Special Edition, usually with commentary, *Carry On Laughing* episode or documentary, picture gallery, trailer etc.

Story: The gist of the plot in a few lines

Notable Lines: Anything that strikes me as being funny, silly or otherwise memorable

Key Scene: Speaks for itself – even the bad *Carry On*s have the odd good moment

Observations: Errors, bloopers or other oddities

All Dragged Up: That moment in a *Carry On* when one or more of the men find an excuse to put on lady's things

Locations: Selective filming sites of interest

Review: Informed opinion and analysis, sometimes irreverent, with general background notes

Verdict: The bottom line and marks out of five

1) Carry On Sergeant (1958)

Cast: Bob Monkhouse (Charlie Sage), Shirley Eaton (Mary Sage), William Hartnell (Sergeant Grimshawe), Eric Barker (Captain Potts), Kenneth Connor (Horace Strong), Charles Hawtrey (Peter Golightly), Kenneth Williams (James Bailey), Terence Longdon (Miles Heywood), Dora Bryan (Norah), Bill Owen (Corporal Bill Copping), Norman Rossington (Herbert Brown), Gerald Campion (Andy Galloway), Hattie Jacques (Captain Clark), Cyril Chamberlain (Gun Sergeant), Anthony Sagar (Stores Sergeant), Alec Bergonzi, Graham Stewart, Alexander Harris, Pat Feeney, Edward Judd, Ronald Clarke, David Williams (Storemen), Gordon Tanner, Frank Forsyth, Basil Dignam, Jack Gatrell, Arnold Diamond, Martin Boddey (Specialists), Ian Whittaker (Medical Corporal), Martin Wyldeck (Mr Sage), Helen Goss (Mary's Mother), Terry Scott (Sergeant Paddy O'Brien), John Mathews (Sergeant Matthews), Ed Devereaux (Sergeant Russell), Leigh Madison (Sheila), Jack Smethurst, Brian Jackson, Don McCorkindale, Leon Eagles, Malcolm Webster, Patrick Durkin, James Villiers, Haydn Ward, Graydon Gould, Jeremy Dempster, Terry Dickenson, Henry Livings, Michael Hunt, Bernard Kay (Recruits)

Crew: Director Gerald Thomas, Screenplay Norman Hudis (based on *The Bull Boys* by RF Delderfield, with additional material by John Antrobus), Producer Peter Rogers, Music Bruce Montgomery, Director of Photography Peter Hennessy, Editor Peter Boita, Art Director Alex Vetchinsky, Assistant Director Geoffrey Haine, Production Manager Frank Bevis, Camera Operator Alan Hume, Continuity Joan Davis, Make-Up Geoffrey Rodway, Hairdresser Stella Rivers, Dress Designer Joan Ellacott, Sound Recordists Robert T MacPhee & Gordon K McCallum, Sound Editor Seymour Logie, Set Dresser Peter Murton, Casting Director Betty White (Anglo Amalgamated, August 1958, b&w, 83m, U)

DVD: 2001 (Studio Canal, D038040)

Story: At Heathercrest National Service Depot, Sergeant Grimshawe (William Hartnell) stands to win £50 if his new recruits form a champion platoon. The only trouble is, they're the most bumbling bunch of no-hopers he's ever seen...

Notable Lines: Kenneth Connor: 'Two of everything you should have and you're in.' / William Hartnell: 'Look at you, standing as if you're pregnant.' Kenneth Williams: 'Wouldn't surprise me, after the way I've been mucked about.' / Kenneth Connor: 'What's there to talk about?' Dora Bryan: 'Life!' Kenneth Connor: 'Life? Infection, decay and death, that's life.' / Dora Bryan: 'We must give ourselves time to know each other. Say about half an hour.'

Key Scene: Like a page from one of Spike Milligan's war memoirs, the scene of the new recruits trying to bayonet a dummy forever sticks in the mind. From mincing Kenneth Williams barely poking a hole in it, to Charles

31

Hawtrey's full-blooded attack ('Let go – do you want to kill someone?' says a concerned William Hartnell), it's all splendid stuff.

Observations: When Bob Monkhouse minces some beef, no meat comes out of the mincer (which probably accounts for the strain on his face).

Location: Queen's Barracks, Stoughton, Surrey.

Review: This is probably the only *Carry On* film that contains incidents that might, just possibly, have happened in real life. Based loosely on army stories by novelist RF Delderfield, *Sergeant* is a taut, efficiently made comic drama with sterling performances by all the cast. William Hartnell, fresh from Granada sitcom *The Army Game*, is the tyrannical sergeant with a heart of gold, Eric Barker the bumbling captain, Bob Monkhouse the lovelorn new recruit, Kenneth Connor the nervous hypochondriac, Charles Hawtrey the comic relief etc. No stereotype is overlooked. But when the performers are this good, it's hard not to be impressed.

Shot in glorious black and white, the film boasts more location filming than most of the other *Carry On*s put together, and even in the Pinewood interiors the parade ground atmosphere is always there in the subtle background sound effects of marching feet and shouted orders. But good though it all is, it's not really a *Carry On* film until Hawtrey and Williams appear. Suddenly the narrative takes a new twist and, with the benefit of hindsight, we're into familiar territory. Hawtrey's effeminacy (somewhat toned down, it has to be said) and Williams' snide upturned nose (he's almost *too* unpleasant here) transform this perfectly reasonable little picture into a bona fide

Carry On outing. The former's hilarious attempt at exercising is only countered by the latter's enviable ability to shin straight up a rope. Dora Bryan is superb as the lovesick waitress and it's a pity she was never used again. Certainly she provides far more screen presence than the vapid Shirley Eaton – chosen presumably for her looks rather than her acting ability.

Sergeant is the most dated of all the *Carry On*s. The basic premise of conscription is alien to us these days, and such expressions as 'I dig' and 'Hey, cat!' – courtesy of guitar-playing Billy Bunter actor Gerald Campion – help push it firmly into pre-*Austin Powers* self-mockery. The teamwork ethos that scriptwriter Norman Hudis espouses also seems worlds away from the internecine warfare of later *Carry On* efforts. But *Sergeant* was made barely a decade after the Second World War and the ability to 'pull together' (now *there's* a double entendre) was seen as crucially important in rebuilding the fabric of society. As the years went by, and the world became a more cynical place, so the films would reflect that.

Verdict: There's no denying *Sergeant* is a tremendously uplifting film and one of the very few *Carry On*s to bring a tear to the eye (or even both). **5/5**.

2) Carry On Nurse (1959)

Cast: Kenneth Connor (Bernie Bishop), Kenneth Williams (Oliver Reckitt), Charles Hawtrey (Humphrey Hinton), Hattie Jacques (Matron), Leslie Phillips (Jack Bell), Shirley Eaton (Nurse Dorothy Denton), Terence Longdon (Ted York), Wilfrid Hyde-White (Colonel), Joan Sims (Nurse Stella Dawson), June Whitfield (Meg), Harry Locke (Mick), Joan Hickson (Sister), Susan Shaw (Jane

Bishop), Bill Owen (Percy Hickson), Irene Handl (Madge Hickson), Brian Oulton (Henry Bray), Hilda Fenemore (Rhoda Bray), Susan Beaumont (Frances James), Susan Stephen (Nurse Georgie Axwell), Cyril Chamberlain (Bert Able), Marianne Stone (Alice Able), Michael Medwin (Ginger), Norman Rossington (Norm), Jill Ireland (Jill Thompson), Ed Devereaux (Alec Lawrence), Frank Forsyth (John Gray), Ann Firbank (Helen Lloyd), John Mathews (Tom Mayhew), Graham Stewart (George Field), Patrick Durkin (Jackson), David Williams (Andrew Newman), Martin Boddey (Perkins), Marita Stanton (Rose Harper), Rosalind Knight (Nurse Nightingale), Leigh Madison (Miss Winn), Stephanie Schiller (New Nurse), Christine Ozanne (Fat Maid), Charles Stanley (Porter), Anthony Sagar (First Ambulance Driver), Fred Griffiths (Second Ambulance Driver), John Van Eyssen (Stephens), Shane Cordell (Attractive Nurse), Jeremy Bishop (Jeremy Connor), Lucy Griffiths (Trolley Lady)

Crew: Director Gerald Thomas, Screenplay Norman Hudis (based on an idea by Patrick Cargill & Jack Beale), Producer Peter Rogers, Music Bruce Montgomery, Director of Photography Reginald Wyer, Editor John Shirley, Art Director Alex Vetchinsky, Assistant Director Stanley Hosgood, Production Manager Frank Bevis, Camera Operator Alan Hume, Continuity Penny Daniels, Make-Up George Blackler, Hairdresser Pearl Orton, Costume Designer Joan Ellacott, Sound Recordists Robert T MacPhee & Bill Daniels, Sound Editor Roger Cherrill, Set Dresser Arthur Taksen, Casting Director Betty White, Nurses' Uniforms by Courtaulds (Anglo Amalgamated, March 1959, b&w, 86m, U/PG)

DVD: 2001 (Studio Canal, D038037)

Story: The ups and downs of life in the King George V men's ward of Haven Hospital…

Notable Lines: Shirley Eaton: 'Mr Bell?' Leslie Phillips: 'Ding dong, you're not wrong.' / Wilfrid Hyde-White: 'Oh dear, sounds as if you don't love me today.' Joan Sims: 'I don't – you're a naughty old buzzer.'

Key Scene: Cyril Chamberlain has the time of his life when he runs around the hospital like a madman after overdosing on some medicine.

Observations: Joan Sims almost pulls the sink unit over as she hurries to turn the taps off. The supposedly coma-tose blood transfusion patient smiles when Rosalind Knight puts her ear to his mouth. At the end, Kenneth Williams is poised to cut into Leslie Phillips' foot, but in the next shot he is back reading his medical book.

All Dragged Up: Charles Hawtrey as a singularly convincing night nurse.

Review: Perhaps it's just me, but I find that most of the *Carry On* medical films are rather overrated, never more so than with *Nurse*. Here the simple plot of *Sergeant* is replaced by a humdrum series of less than hilarious medical incidents. There's little by way of storyline to carry any of the events along, and (Charles Hawtrey aside) most of the regulars give muted performances; Kenneth Williams hardly utters a word, but when he does he plays his part totally straight, falling for the delectable Jill Ireland (well, she'd turn anyone straight). We do get plenty of jokes about the male member and the chance to see Terence Longdon in the buff, so I suppose it makes a change from seeing nurses in their underwear. Oh, actually we do, and tied to a bed as well. There's kinky.

Nurse is a sentimental film – note the scene in which Kenneth Connor discovers he won't be able to box again – with some occasional comedy moments. As such, it is different to almost every other *Carry On* film, even *Sergeant*, which was obviously a comedy from the start. Certainly there are some good moments, but we have to sit through much turgid scene-setting before we get to them. One of the best-known sequences is Kenneth Williams taking a group of patients to the operating theatre to do a spot of DIY bunion-removing. Poor Leslie Phillips is the victim and the combination of doom-laden music and Kenneth Williams' manic grin ('Look, stop mucking about!') sets the tone for a nightmarish sequence of black humour. And then of course there's the very final moment with the daffodil, which is priceless. But these two scenes do not a comedy make.

Verdict: *Nurse* is one of the least interesting black and white outings – my diagnosis is **2/5**.

3) Carry On Teacher (1959)

Cast: Ted Ray (William Wakefield), Charles Hawtrey (Michael Bean), Kenneth Connor (Gregory Adams), Kenneth Williams (Edwin Milton), Leslie Phillips (Alistair Grigg), Hattie Jacques (Grace Short), Joan Sims (Sarah Allcock), Rosalind Knight (Felicity Wheeler), Cyril Chamberlain (Alf), Richard O'Sullivan (Robin Stevens), Roy Hines (Harry Bird), George Howell (Billy Haig), Diana Beevers (Penelope Lee), Jacqueline Lewis (Pat Gordon), Carol White (Sheila Dale), Paul Cole (Atkins), Larry Dann (Desperate Boy)

Crew: Director Gerald Thomas, Screenplay Norman Hudis, Producer Peter Rogers, Music Bruce Montgomery, Director of Photography Reginald Wyer, Editor John Shirley, Art Director Lionel Couch, Assistant Director Bert Batt, Production Manager Frank Bevis, Camera Operator Alan Hume, Continuity Tilly Day, Make-Up George Blackler, Hairdresser Olga Angelinetta, Costume Designer Laurell Staffell, Sound Recordists Robert T MacPhee & Gordon K McCallum, Sound Editor Leslie Wiggins, Set Dresser Terence Morgan, Casting Director Betty White (Anglo Amalgamated, August 1959, b&w, 86m, U)

DVD: 2001 (Studio Canal, D038042)

Story: Headmaster William Wakefield (Ted Ray) dreams of retiring to a modern school in the country. But he can only do that if his school passes a rigorous inspection headed by child psychologist Alistair Grigg (Leslie Phillips) – and his pupils seem determined to scupper his plans...

Notable Lines: Kenneth Williams: 'Extraordinary theory. You bend a child double in order to give it an upright character.' / Charles Hawtrey: 'Noxious ninny!' / Rosalind Knight: 'Are you satisfied with your equipment, Miss Allcock?' Joan Sims: 'Well, I've had no complaints so far.' / Joan Sims: 'They've taken the pea!' / George Howell: 'We're doing Modern History, sir. That's full of bangs.' / Leslie Phillips: 'Free expression is just the thing for other people's children.'

Key Scene: It has to be the beautifully choreographed itching powder fiasco. The teachers are sitting in the staff

37

room trying to play down the hysteria that is erupting all around them, when Leslie Phillips, almost unnoticed, starts scratching himself. Next, Joan Sims. Then Kenneths Connor and Williams – and suddenly they're all doing it. Phillips' performance as he rubs desperately at his stomach is hilarious – quite the funniest thing in the film – and Hattie Jacques' single involuntary shriek is expertly timed. The sequence even adds depth to the characters, as we witness Kenneth Williams' true feelings for Hawtrey's music teacher at last: 'Shut up, you jackass!' he berates him, as Hawtrey falls into the fireplace. It ends, in the only way it could, with a roomful of lurching, grimacing actors doing a conga round the table.

Observations: The film reveals that toluene and nitric acid make TNT, while sulphur, potassium, nitrate and carbon are the chief ingredients for a bomb (but don't try this at home, children). One scene refers to a 'Bowdlerized' version of *Romeo and Juliet*, a reference to moral guardian Thomas Bowdler (1754–1825), who went through the entire works of Shakespeare deleting all the bits that shouldn't 'be read aloud in a family'. Twit.

Location: Drayton Green Primary School, Ealing, London (formerly Drayton Combined School).

Review: Only three films into its run, the *Carry On*s have hit on a winning formula – the only difference between *Teacher* and *Sergeant* is that the crusty figure of authority is up against children instead of soldiers. *Teacher* is one of the few *Carry On* films to feature juveniles and here, led by 15-year-old Richard (*Man About the House*) O'Sullivan, they dominate the proceedings. Compared with them, the regulars seem quite sensible. Kenneth Williams is the liberal English teacher, Joan Sims the 'jolly hockey sticks' gym mistress and Kenneth Connor the serious, academic science master (albeit lovelorn as usual). Even German-speaking Leslie Phillips gives a near-naturalistic performance. Charles Hawtrey (playing Mr Bean!) is the closest to a figure of fun – with his mortarboard, billowing gown and squinty pebble glasses, he could have stepped out of an old Will Hay comedy (easy enough, as Hawtrey featured in several). His impressive piano introduction to 'Ten Green Bottles' is matched only by his extraordinary body language as he conducts his execrable *Romeo and Juliet* musical score. ('If music be the food of love, belt up!' exclaims Kenneth Connor with feeling.)

Teacher is also one of the darkest *Carry On*s. The pupils' psychological warfare against their teachers is intense and the various references to terrorist activities and home-made bombs strike an uncomfortable chord in these post 9/11 days (witness Hawtrey's reaction to the ticking 'bomb'). Of course, at the end everything is seen to be just a ruse to keep Wakefield on, and in true *Dead Poets Society* style, the pupils unanimously declare their love for their Headmaster in a scene that should bring a tear to the throat and a lump to the eye. But thankfully there is one final joke to dissipate the cloying sentimentality: Kenneth Williams and Charles Hawtrey go to hug Hattie Jacques but accidentally embrace each other, immediately backing away in joint disgust.

Verdict: An old-fashioned comedy with old-fashioned sentiments, I give this '*Sergeant* in civvies' **4/5** (could do better).

4) Carry On Constable (1960)

Cast: Sid James (Sergeant Frank Wilkins), Eric Barker (Inspector Mills), Kenneth Connor (Constable Charlie Constable), Kenneth Williams (PC Stanley Benson), Charles Hawtrey (PC Timothy Gorse), Leslie Phillips (PC Tom Potter), Joan Sims (WPC Gloria Passworthy), Hattie Jacques (Sergeant Laura Moon), Cyril Chamberlain (Thurston), Shirley Eaton (Sally Barry), Terence Longdon (Herbert Hall), Joan Hickson (Mrs May), Irene Handl (Distraught Woman), Jill Adams (WPC Harrison), Freddie Mills (Crook), Brian Oulton (Store Manager), Robin Ray (Assistant Manager), Esma Cannon (Deaf Woman), Victor Maddern (Criminal Type), Joan Young (Suspect), Hilda Fenemore (Agitated Woman), Noel Dyson (Vague Woman), Michael Balfour (Matt), Diane Aubrey (Honoria), Ian Curry (Eric), Mary Law (Shop Assistant), Lucy Griffiths (Miss Horton), Peter Bennett (Thief), Jack Taylor (Cliff), Eric Boon (Shorty), Janetta Lake (Girl with Dog), Dorinda Stevens (Young Woman), Tom Gill, Frank Forsyth, John Antrobus, Eric Corrie (Citizens)

Crew: Director Gerald Thomas, Screenplay Norman Hudis (based on an idea by Brock Williams), Producer Peter Rogers, Music Bruce Montgomery, Director of Photography Ted Scaife, Editor John Shirley, Art Director Carmen Dillon, Assistant Director Peter Manley, Production Manager Frank Bevis, Camera Operator Alan Hume, Continuity Joan Davis, Make-Up George Blackler, Dress Designer Yvonne Caffin, Hairdresser Stella Rivers, Sound Recordists Robert T MacPhee & Bill Daniels, Sound Editor Leslie Wiggins, Set Dresser Vernon Dixon, Casting Director Betty White (Anglo Amalgamated, February 1960, b&w, 86m, U)

DVD: 2001 (Studio Canal, D038033)

Story: When the staff of a police station come down with flu, Sergeant Frank Wilkins (Sid James) has to rely on four incompetent recruits to further his promotion...

Notable Lines: Eric Barker: 'Would you care to have a look at my cherbunkin?' Sid James: 'If it'll give you satisfaction.' / Charles Hawtrey: 'You merry quipper, you!'

Key Scene: When Charles Hawtrey minces into the police station with birdcage and bunch of flowers held aloft, proffering the immortal catchphrase, 'Oh *hello*!', he is so extraordinarily *gay* that the other actors just gawp at him open-mouthed. It's arguably his most overtly camp entrance into a *Carry On* film ever, and he cannot top the scene for the rest of the movie (although his weird jump off the stairwell at the end comes perilously close).

Observations: When Sid James receives a drenching with a bucket of water, poor old Cyril Chamberlain standing behind him gets soaked too.

All Dragged Up: Charles Hawtrey and Kenneth Williams dress up as female shoppers to lure a pickpocket.

Location: Ealing, London.

Review: The first truly plotless *Carry On* effort, *Constable* introduces a dry patch for the series that wouldn't end until *Cabby* in 1963. Relying more on slapstick than wit (someone slips on a banana skin – that's how sophisticated it is) the film gives only cursory acknowledgement to the archetypical Hudis storyline of 'officer relying on duff new recruits'. Instead, the audience is presented with a disconnected series of comic set pieces, culminating in a finale involving the capture of a gang of robbers – therefore proving that these raw recruits aren't as incompetent as they seem.

Most of the cast are clearly treading water until something better comes along. Charles Hawtrey alone manages to rise above the material, stepping out of the narrative to comment on other characters' lines ('Oh, priceless innuendo – how witty'). Of course, this is the film that introduces Sid James to the fold and as such it should be worth remembering, but his performance here is surprisingly uncharismatic – he's a notably watered-down version of the lecherous Cockney geezer he would soon become. To add to the flatness of his performance, James' first scene with Eric Barker looks completely unrehearsed – the jokes lack punchlines, while Barker seems to have lost his place in the script.

On the plus side, Irene Handl is superb (delivering, a decade ahead of Mrs Slocombe, one of the few 'pussy' gags in the *Carry On* canon), and there are some nice walk-on parts for Victor Maddern and Esma Cannon. There's also the infamous shower scene, featuring the sight of four naked men covering their modesty with towels. Add to this the naked backside of Shirley Eaton in the bath and the series' reputation for risqué scenes starts here. In fact, you wouldn't see another bare male backside until the nudist flick in *Carry On Camping* almost a decade later, and you'd have to wait until 1975 to see Kenneth Williams bare his again, in the appropriately named *Carry On Behind*. Ultimately, though, the film doesn't quite know whether it's gritty realism or knockabout comedy. As Kenneth Williams wrote in his diary in February 1960, the film was 'mediocre & tired. I think everyone knew it.'

Verdict: As a lazy attempt to keep the formula going for its own sake, it really only deserves **2/5**.

5) Carry On Regardless (1961)

Cast: Sid James (Bert Handy), Kenneth Connor (Sam Twist), Kenneth Williams (Francis Courtenay), Charles Hawtrey (Gabriel Dimple), Joan Sims (Lily Duveen), Liz Fraser (Delia King), Terence Longdon (Montgomery Infield-Hopping), Bill Owen (Mike Weston), Esma Cannon (Miss Cooling), Stanley Unwin (Landlord), Fenella Fielding (Penny Panting), Ed Devereaux (Ed Panting), Cyril Chamberlain (Policeman), Ambrosine Phillpotts (Yoki's Owner), Molly Weir (Bird Owner), Eric Pohlmann (Sinister Man), June Jago (Nurse), Hattie Jacques (Sister), Joan Hickson (Matron), Norman Rossington (Referee), Terence Alexander (Trevor Trelawney), Julia Arnall (Trudy Trelawney), Jerry Desmonde (Martin Paul), Jimmy Thompson (Mr Delling), Carole Shelley (Helen Delling), Tony Sagar (Bus Conductor), Fred Griffiths (Cab Driver), Howard Marion Crawford (Wine Organizer), Bernard Hunter (Customer), Kynaston Reeves (Testy Old Man), Fraser Kerr (Houseman), Douglas Ives (Patient), Maureen Moore (Probationer), Victor Maddern (First Sinister Passenger), Denis Shaw (Second Sinister passenger), Betty Marsden ('Mata Hari'), Freddie Mills (Lefty), Tom Clegg (Massive Micky McGee), Joe Robinson (Dynamite Dan), Lucy Griffiths (Auntie), Ian Whittaker (Shop Assistant), Jack Taylor (MC/Policeman), George Street (Club Receptionist), Sydney Tafler (Strip Club Manager), Cyril Raymond (Army Officer), Nancy Roberts (Old Lady), Charles Julian (Old Man in Ruby Room), Michael Ward (Photographer), Ian Wilson (Advertiser), Madame Yang

(Chinese Lady), Judith Furse (Formidable Lady), David Stoll (Distraught Manager), Ian Curry (Leonard Beamish)

Crew: Director Gerald Thomas, Screenplay Norman Hudis, Producer Peter Rogers, Music Bruce Montgomery, Director of Photography Alan Hume, Editor John Shirley, Art Director Lionel Couch, Assistant Director Jack Causey, Unit Manager Claude Watson, Camera Operator Dudley Lovell, Continuity Gladys Goldsmith, Make-Up George Blackler, Hairdresser Biddy Chrystal, Costume Designer Joan Ellacott, Sound Recordists Robert T MacPhee & Gordon McCallum, Sound Editor Arthur Ridout, Casting Director Betty White (Anglo Amalgamated, March 1961, 90m, U)

DVD: 2001 (Studio Canal, D038038)

Story: Bert Handy (Sid James) and Miss Cooling (Esma Cannon) manage the Helping Hands agency – an organisation that sends people out to do jobs. And that's it.

Notable Lines: Bernard Hunter: 'Madam, for you a soupçon?' Joan Sims: 'Oh really, what kind of soup?' / Kynaston Reeves: 'Do you provide substitutes?' Esma Cannon: 'No! This is a respectable firm!' / Charles Hawtrey: 'Blue tits… have you got any?' Sydney Tafler: 'No, this place is centrally heated.' / Kenneth Williams: 'He said you can pull down the greenhouse, the outhouse, the wash-house and the –' Kenneth Connor: 'And that fell down of its own accord.'

Key Scene: The bit where Kenneth Williams, as an interpreter, is drawn into a heated argument between English husband Terence Alexander and fiery German wife Julia

Arnell is a masterpiece of comic timing. He begins calmly but then as he's sucked into the situation, he sides more and more with Arnell until he assumes her personality and starts arguing with her husband. Williams' range of emotions here is formidable. Forget about comedy acting, this is just great acting full stop.

Observations: Stanley Unwin appears to blaspheme at the end of one of his 'gobbledegook' lines. There's a suspiciously racist comment about Chinese people ('Wonder if it's true what they say?'). Julia Arnell is actually shouting in genuine, albeit old-fashioned, German – for instance, 'You know what you are? You are a very mean and disgusting shabby bloke! I think you understand me very well – out you go!'

Location: Windsor, Berks.

Review: Another plotless film, although at least this time it makes a feature of it with a series of 20 (count them) sketches involving various members of the team. Some of them work – Kenneth Williams' charming interlude with Yoki the chimp or Joan Sims getting sloshed at a posh wine-tasting party – while others are unfunny to begin with and quickly outstay their welcome, in particular the *Thirty Nine Steps* spoof or the antics at the Ideal Home Exhibition. Kenneth Connor's attempt to give up smoking is embarrassingly overplayed, while the less said about his laughing butler the better. Scriptwriter Norman Hudis obviously had all these vaguely promising ideas but didn't know how to incorporate them into a proper narrative, so he just strung them all together and pretended it made some sort of sense. But it's as unsatisfying as sketch films always are – compare the conveyer belt of skits that is *Monty Python and the Holy Grail* with the well-structured narrative of their far superior *Life of Brian*. No contest.

Of course, *Regardless* has its good points. One of them is the late lamented presence of Stanley Unwin, whose 'gobbledegook' adds a touch of vitality that the film otherwise lacks ('How do you do? Mind if I interprey?' asks Kenneth Williams). And the final scene of chaos as the Helping Hands team tries to clean up Unwin's old house – only to demolish it in the process – is funny stuff, despite looking like a page out of *The Beano*. In the meantime, keep an eye out for Nicholas Parsons (who looks the same now as he did then – unless he's died since this went to press) and the gorgeous Fenella Fielding in cameo roles. At least in a film this episodic you get more British character actors for your money than usual, but it's small consolation for a very disappointing effort.

Verdict: Kenneth Williams in his diary entry for Friday, 17 March 1961 notes this film was 'quite terrible. An unmitigated disaster.' Well, I wouldn't go that far, but for being deeply unsatisfying, despite the nurses in their undies, I give it a mere **2/5**.

6) Carry On Cruising (1962)

Cast: Sid James (Captain Wellington Crowther), Kenneth Williams (Leonard Marjoribanks), Kenneth Connor (Dr Arthur Binn), Lance Percival (Wilfred Haines), Liz Fraser (Glad Trimble), Dilys Laye (Flo Castle), Esma Cannon (Bridget Madderley), Cyril Chamberlain (Tom Tree), Jimmy Thompson (Sam Turner), Ronnie Stevens (Drunk), Vincent Ball (Jenkins), Willoughby Goddard (Fat Man), Ed Devereaux (Young Officer), Brian Rawlinson

(Steward), Anton Rodgers (Young Man), Tony Sagar (First Cook), Mario Fabrizi (Second Cook), Terence Holland (Passerby), Evan David (Bridegroom), Marian Collins (Bride), Jill Mai Meredith (Shapely Miss), Alan Casley (Seaman)

Crew: Director Gerald Thomas, Screenplay Norman Hudis (from a story by Eric Barker), Producer Peter Rogers, Music Bruce Montgomery & Douglas Gamley, Director of Photography Alan Hume, Editor John Shirley, Art Director Carmen Dillon, Assistant Director Jack Causey, Production Manager Bill Hill, Camera Operator Dudley Lovell, Continuity Penny Daniels, Make-Up George Blackler & Geoff Rodway, Hairdresser Biddy Chrystal, Costume Designer Joan Ellacott, Sound Recordists Robert T MacPhee & Bill Daniels, Sound Editors Arthur Ridout & Archie Ludski, Casting Director Betty White, Beachwear for Miss Fraser & Miss Laye by Silhouette (Anglo Amalgamated, April 1962, Eastmancolor, 89m, U)

DVD: 2001 (Studio Canal, D038035)

Story: En route for Spain, Italy and North Africa on the SS *Happy Wanderer*, Captain Wellington Crowther (Sid James) wants a relaxing final voyage before promotion. But with a bunch of new recruits on board, things don't look promising…

Notable Lines: Kenneth Connor: 'I'll massage your clavicles.' Sid James: 'You will not!' / Kenneth Connor: 'Would you like to poop up on the pop-deck with me?' Dilys Laye: 'Doctor, do me a favour – operate somewhere else.' / Ronnie Stevens: 'That's why I drink – to forget her.'

Kenneth Connor: 'Who?' Ronnie Stevens: 'Blessed if I can remember.' / Kenneth Connor: 'This afternoon I fight 15 bulls.' Kenneth Williams: 'That's an awful lot of bull.' / Sid James: 'Flo, ebb a little.' / Sid James: 'This bloke Freud knew what he was talking about. On the other hand, I'm not a Jung man.' Kenneth Williams: 'As long as you're Jung at heart!' / Lance Percival: 'Blimey, smells like a Babylon boozer's bedroom!'

Key Scene: It has to be the bit when they've all come aboard from Spain, and Kenneth Connor is dressed as a matador. Some ribald jokes (see above) are swiftly followed by Kenneth Williams' gleeful impression of a charging bull – making it clear that these are just school-boys let loose in an adult world.

Observations: There's a ropey cut when Kenneth Connor sprays Sid James with the soda siphon – in close-up he's holding Sid's head, in the long shot he isn't. When Sid experiments with making a cocktail, the volume and colour of the discarded drink in the flower vase changes dramatically between shots.

Review: The last Norman Hudis script, and thankfully the last 'new recruits make their boss livid before showing him how much they love him' plot. *Cruising* is also the first of the series shot in colour. But while the film bene-fits from this extra gloss, it loses any kudos because of its studio-bound setting. For a storyline that features exotic foreign locales, the lack of same makes the film look cheap. The location filming (for which P&O is thanked in the credits) is limited to a few brief moments at the start, but these end up looking like stock footage shots and their inclusion makes little impact.

CARRY ON FILMS

Concentrating on the amorous experiences of the various crewmembers, the *Love Boat*-style storyline chugs along quite nicely, albeit lacking any great set pieces. Kenneth Connor is more assured than usual – his impression of Kenneth Williams' laugh is uncannily accurate, and he is allowed that rare privilege of addressing the audience and, even more rare, bursting into song (which, it must be said, he does with a certain aplomb). And at last Sid James and Kenneth Williams are allowed to interact properly for the first time, even though their main topic of discussion is the then-fashionable study of psychoanalysis! Lance Percival, standing in for Charles Hawtrey, gives a commendable performance as the incompetent ship's cook. It's a pity he never returned to the fold, as his dry performance here suggests he would have fitted in perfectly. He is also allowed a rare in-joke, when he comments on the fact that director Gerald Thomas never once sways his cameras to suggest a shipboard setting: 'These stabilisers are wonderful!' he chirps gaily.

Sid James coasts through the whole thing in a restrained world-weary performance that makes it obvious how much his character yearns to be back on dry land with his wife and prize begonias. With references to his advancing years (Liz Fraser calls Dilys Laye's infatuation with him a 'Dad fad'), he's far removed from the 'Jack the lad' he would become from the next film onwards.

Verdict: Cheap and slow-moving, it may be one of the lesser *Carry Ons*, but some quick-fire repartee ('Who?' 'Me.' 'You?' 'Aye.' 'Come!') and solid playing by the regulars combine to make this a watertight **3/5**.

49

7) Carry On Cabby (1963)

Cast: Sid James (Charlie Hawkins), Hattie Jacques (Peggy Hawkins), Charles Hawtrey (Terry 'Pintpot' Tankard), Kenneth Connor (Ted Watson), Liz Fraser (Sally), Bill Owen (Smiley), Esma Cannon (Flo Sims), Jim Dale (Expectant Father), Milo O'Shea (Len), Judith Furse (Battleaxe), Renee Houston (Molly), Cyril Chamberlain (Sarge), Norman Chappell (Allbright), Amanda Barrie (Anthea), Carole Shelley (Dumb Driver), Ambrosine Phillpotts (Aristocratic Lady), Michael Ward (Tweeds Man), Noel Dyson (District Nurse), Norman Mitchell (First Businessman), Michael Nightingale (Second Businessman), Peter Gilmore (Dancy), Darryl Kavann (Punchy), Don McCorkindale (Tubby), Ian Wilson (Clerk), Marion Collins (Bride), Peter Byrne (Bridegroom), Charles Stanley (Geoff), Peter Jesson (Car Salesman), Frank Forsyth (Chauffeur), Valerie Van Ost, Marian Horton (Glamcab Drivers)

Crew: Director Gerald Thomas, Screenplay Talbot Rothwell (based on an original idea by SC Green & RM Hills), Producer Peter Rogers, Music Eric Rogers, Director of Photography Alan Hume, Editor Archie Ludski, Art Director Jack Stephens, Assistant Director Peter Bolton, Unit Manager Donald Toms, Associate Producer Frank Bevis, Camera Operator Godfrey Godar, Continuity Penny Daniels, Make-Up Geoffrey Rodway & Jim Hydes, Hairdresser Biddy Chrystal, Costume Designer Joan Ellacott, Sound Recordists Bill Daniels & Gordon K McCallum, Sound Editor Arthur Ridout (Anglo Amalgamated, June 1963, b&w, 91m, U)

DVD: 2001 (Studio Canal, D038031)

Story: In Balham, Charlie and Peggy Hawkins (Sid James and Hattie Jacques) engage in a no-holds-barred battle over whose taxi company will pull in the most fares...

Notable Lines: Kenneth Connor: 'Now my advice to you is B off.' Charles Hawtrey: 'You mean, buzz off.' Kenneth Connor: 'No, but you're getting warm.' / Sid James: 'In no time at all you'll find you're about as popular as a wickerwork seat in a nudist camp. And you know what sort of impression that makes on people.' / Hattie Jacques: 'Even when we get a chance to talk, it's cabs, cabs, cabs. He can't even get into bed now without saying "Where to?"' / Hattie Jacques (weighing herself): 'Who would have thought a towel would have made all that difference?' / Jim Dale: 'Are you a taxi?' Sid James: 'No. This is a taxi, I'm a driver, he's a learner and you're a twit.' / Esma Cannon: 'Men? They're only good for one thing. And they wouldn't be much good without us.' / Charles Hawtrey: 'She was covered all over in legs and things.' Sid James: 'Don't be filthy!' / Sid James: 'Plastic gas mask holders – that's brilliant. All we need now is some plastic gas.'

Key Scene: There's a lovely little moment when Jim Dale's wife gives birth in the back of Sid James' cab. Dale, Hawtrey and James puff away nervously at their cigarettes while executing a complex pacing routine outside the cab. When the midwife announces the new arrival, all three shout out, 'We're daddies!'

Observations: At one point Charles Hawtrey says, 'I wonder what it's like to have a baby?' He would discover a few years later as 'phantom pregnancy' husband Mr Barron in *Carry On Doctor*. In a break from tradition, the opening titles appear over the first scene rather than on separate title cards (a technique repeated in *Spying* and *Emmannuelle*).

All Dragged Up: Kenneth Connor in Glamcabs garb.

Locations: Windsor town centre, Berks; Iver Heath and Black Park, Bucks.

Review: In his second and final *Carry On* appearance, *Last of the Summer Wine* actor Bill Owen shows us what he can bring to the craft of comedy acting – absolutely nothing. But apart from him, this is a great film, with brilliant performances by all the cast, and a fast, witty script by Talbot Rothwell, the first of 20 he would write for the series.

The omission of Kenneth Williams (he hated the script – so what's new?) goes largely unnoticed in this extremely well-played and well-written satire on big-business ethics and the eternal war between the sexes. Jacques is extremely good as the frustrated housewife who gets her own back on her work-obsessed husband by forming a rival all-female cab company, along with diminutive Esma Cannon. Sid James gets his best part yet as the fully rounded Cockney wide boy with a scam up each sleeve (and both trouser legs), although the twist here – unlike most of the later films – is that he's a faithful husband and doesn't want to play the field. (Of course, he never gets the opportunity…) Charles Hawtrey is excellent as the learner driver who keeps getting in Sid James' way ('Ooh, I could punish myself!' he exclaims crossly).

War imagery is to the fore here, with both sides planning their campaigns with military efficiency. Neither side is averse to a bit of sabotage – Hawtrey is only employed because he's an ex-serviceman and Liz Fraser is labelled a fifth columnist for displaying a copy of the all-female Glamcabs poster in Sid James' garage. The climactic ending, in which the combined forces of the taxi companies rout some nasty criminal types headed by Peter Gilmore (the first of many villainous parts he would play in the series) resembles a wartime thriller, with uncharacteristically atmospheric direction by Gerald Thomas. It may go on too long and it's as tacked-on as the ending to *Carry On Constable*, but it adds a frisson of reality to the proceedings.

Verdict: Rothwell Talbot's first script is a welcome breath of fresh air for a series that was beginning to look rather stale, so I give it a healthy **5/5**.

8) Carry On Jack (1963)

Cast: Bernard Cribbins (Midshipman Albert Poop-Decker), Kenneth Williams (Captain Fearless), Charles Hawtrey (Walter Sweetley), Juliet Mills (Sally), Donald Houston (Lieutenant Jonathan Howett), Percy Herbert (Mr Angel), Jim Dale (Young Sedan Chair Carrier), Ian Wilson (Old Sedan Chair Carrier), Patrick Cargill (Spanish Governor), Cecil Parker (First Sealord), Frank Forsyth (Second Sealord), John Brooking (Third Sealord), Peter Gilmore (Patch), Ed Devereaux (Hook), Jimmy Thompson (Nelson), Anton Rodgers (Hardy), Michael Nightingale (Town Crier), Barrie Gosney (Coach Driver), Jan Muzurus (Spanish Captain), Vivian Ventura (Spanish Secretary), Marianne Stone, Sally Douglas, Dorinda Stevens, Jennifer Hill, Rosemary Manley, Dominique Don, Marian Collins, Jean Hamilton (Girls at Dirty Dicks)

Crew: Director Gerald Thomas, Screenplay Talbot Rothwell, Producer Peter Rogers, Music Eric Rogers, Director of Photography Alan Hume, Editor Archie Ludski, Art Director Jack Shampan, Assistant Director Anthony Waye, Unit Manager Donald Toms, Associate Producer Frank Bevis, Camera Operator Godfrey Godar, Continuity Penny Daniels, Make-Up Geoffrey Rodway & Jim Hydes, Hairdresser Olga Angelinetta, Costume Designer Joan Ellacott, Sound Recordist Bill Daniels, Sound Editor Christopher Lancaster, Technical Advisor Ian Cox (Anglo Amalgamated, November 1963, Eastmancolor, 91m, A/PG)

DVD: 2001 (Studio Canal, D038036)

Story: In the Napoleonic Wars, Captain Fearless (Kenneth Williams) and his motley crew battle against rebellious sailors and hostile pirates…

Notable Lines: Bernard Cribbins (about a sedan chair): 'Must be dreadful carrying this great heavy thing day after day.' Jim Dale: 'Well, it's better than walking the streets, isn't it?' / Bernard Cribbins: 'Before I left home my mother warned me that things like this might happen to me. I must write and thank her.' / Kenneth Williams: 'My boy, you can look after my old cow.' Bernard Cribbins: 'Sir, I'm a midshipman, not a lady's maid!' / Donald Houston: 'Look sir, the plate on the deck – that's where her last captain fell.' Kenneth Williams: 'I'm not surprised. I nearly tripped over the wretched thing myself.' / Kenneth Williams: 'I don't like the idea of leaving Emma (the cow) behind.' Bernard Cribbins: 'Don't worry sir, Spain's full of bulls – she'll love it.' Kenneth Williams: 'Love what?' Bernard Cribbins: 'Bull.' Kenneth Williams: 'I hope so.'

Charles Hawtrey (to camera): 'She'd be a stupid cow if she didn't!' / Bernard Cribbins: 'Do you mean to say he plighted your thingummy when you were only 13?' Juliet Mills: 'Yes.' Bernard Cribbins: 'Dirty rotten plighter.'

Key Scene: The best bit in the film – and that's not saying much – is when Donald Houston tells Kenneth Williams to throw the book at Bernard Cribbins. Bang goes the heavy volume into Cribbins' arms, and when Houston demands a more severe retribution, Williams says aghast, 'You mean you want me to punish him *more*?'

All Dragged Up: Juliet Mills as Walter Sweetley.

Location: Frensham Pond, Surrey.

Review: Oh dear, what can I say? Let me just put it like this – *Carry On Jack* is without doubt one of the most boring films I've ever had the misfortune to sit through. Yes, it's even duller than Steven Soderbergh's *Traffic* – hard to believe, but there it is. The funny thing is, I remember watching it when I was seven or eight and being absolutely *enthralled*. It had everything: pirates, galleons, walking the plank, sea battles and sawing someone's leg off, not to mention the exciting suggestion that a woman might take her clothes off. And then I watched it last week and got a real shock. I sat there in a semi-stupor, not quite crediting the sheer banality of it all. How could I have ever enjoyed this limp effort? It's not that it's particularly bad, it's just that it is so damned *boring*. Talbot Rothwell's second script began life as a non-*Carry On* film, but even then it was supposed to be a comedy, and that's the one key element that's missing from this woeful mess.

There are four main problems with *Carry On Jack*. 1)

There is only one woman character in it, and half the time she's supposed to be a man. This means that the all-male cast is a real stumbling-block for the *Carry On* stock-in-trade of sexual double entendres. 2) Donald Houston and Percy Herbert entertain the strange notion that they're acting in a serious film. Or rather, a serious tenth-rate melodrama. And they have many scenes together in this film. Very many. 3) There is a complete over-reliance on stock footage, which leads to the absurd situation that the most impressive scenes in *Carry On Jack* come from another film. (I wish I knew which one – I'd much rather have watched that.) 4) Far from being plotless, the film has so much plot that very often there's no room for the humour. Kenneth Williams noted in his diary that 'the editing was all wrong for comedy' and he's right.

Bernard Cribbins and Kenneth Williams try their best, but the deadweight scripting gets them every time. Even Charles Hawtrey gives a bad performance – for some insane reason, he's playing a *character*, rather than himself, and so his comedic presence is immediately stifled. The less said about Jim Dale the better.

I suppose technically it's not bad. The camera moves up and down during the ship scenes, mimicking a sea swell, while the sets are generally convincing. And the opening tableau of Nelson's death scene is quite clever. But clever isn't funny, and when you can't even manage to raise a smile when putting a cow into a lifeboat, you haven't got a hope.

Verdict: For committing the cardinal sin of being as dull as ditchwater, it gets a washed-up **1/5**.

'What a Send Up!' (1964–1972)

9) Carry On Spying (1964)

Cast: Eric Barker (The Chief), Kenneth Williams (Desmond Simkins), Barbara Windsor (Daphne Honeybutt), Charles Hawtrey (Charlie Bind), Bernard Cribbins (Harold Crump), Jim Dale (Carstairs), Richard Wattis (Cobley), Dilys Laye (Lila), Victor Maddern (Milchmann), Judith Furse (Dr Crow), Eric Pohlmann (The Fat Man), Renee Houston (Madame), John Bluthal (Headwaiter), Tom Clegg (Doorman), Gertan Klauber (Code Clerk), Norman Mitchell (Policeman), Hugh Futcher (Bed Of Nails Man), Frank Forsyth (Professor Stark), Derek Sydney (Algerian Man), Jill Mai Meredith (Cigarette Girl), Angela Ellison (Cloakroom Girl), Norah Gordon (Elderly Woman), Jack Taylor, Bill Cummings (Thugs), Anthony Baird, Patrick Durkin (Guards), Virginia Tyler, Judi Johnson, Gloria Best (Funhouse Girls), Audrey Wilson, Vicky Smith, Jane Lumb, Marian Collins, Sally Douglas, Christine Rodgers, Maya Koumani (Amazon Guards)

Crew: Director Gerald Thomas, Screenplay Talbot Rothwell & Sid Colin, Producer Peter Rogers, Music Eric Rogers ('Too Late' by Alex Alstone & Geoffrey Parsons, 'The Magic of Love' by Eric Rogers), Director of Photography Alan Hume, Editor Archie Ludski, Art

Director Alex Vetchinsky, Assistant Director Peter Bolton, Unit Manager Donald Toms, Associate Producer Frank Bevis, Camera Operator Godfrey Godar, Continuity Penny Daniels, Make-Up WT Partleton, Hairdresser Biddy Chrystal, Costume Designer Yvonne Caffin, Sound Recordists CC Stevens & Bill Daniels, Sound Editor Christopher Lancaster (Anglo Amalgamated, Film Company, June 1964, b&w, 87m, A/U)

DVD: 2001 (Studio Canal, D038041)

Story: The Chief of the Secret Service (Eric Barker) sends his team of untried secret agents to find the Fat Man, head of the Society for the Total Extinction of Nonconforming Humans (STENCH)…

Notable Lines: Kenneth Williams: 'Number?' Charles Hawtrey: 'Double O, oooh.' Kenneth Williams: 'O what?' Charles Hawtrey: 'Well, I have no idea. They looked at me and they said, "Oh-oh, oooh!"' / Bernard Cribbins: 'I'd like a packet of filter-tipped matches, please.' Jim Dale: 'I'm sorry, I've only got filter-tipped bootlaces.' Bernard Cribbins: 'I can't smoke them. They make me deaf.' / Eric Barker: 'Emile Fuzak, known as The Fat Man. Description: Male. Fat.' / Jim Dale: 'Now, come on, hand it over or I'll shoot you where you sit.' Barbara Windsor: 'Oh no, not where he sits!'

Key Scene: For the closest the series ever got to *The Goons*, it has to be the bit where Bernard Cribbins approaches a beard-wearing Jim Dale selling matches. Their unlikely exchange of coded lines (see above) is pure Spike Milligan.

Observations: On the 'Funhouse', the inside of the door doesn't have the peephole that we can see on the outside. (And inside there are Sega fruit machines – my, this is a den of iniquity.) Sound effects used in Barbara Windsor's interrogation scene would reappear in the 1966 film *Dr Who and the Daleks*.

All Dragged Up: Bernard Cribbins as a belly dancer.

Review: After the doldrums of *Carry On Jack*, we're back on course with this fantastic spoof of all things James Bond. Star of the piece is Kenneth Williams, who adopts full 'smarmy' mode to present us with a far more sympathetic and amusing character than his previous smug and supercilious roles ever allowed him to be. From now on, he would be just as infantile and incompetent as the rest of the *Carry On*ers. His hilarious delivery of 'No, don't be like that, Chief!' is straight out of *Hancock's Half-Hour* and the film's all the better for it. Bernard Cribbins is as reliable as ever and new girl Barbara Windsor looks absolutely stunning. She's also portrayed as the most intelligent of the bunch, with a photographic memory, so that obviously excuses her gyrating around in belly-dancing gear. And any film in which Jim Dale is asked to play his role straight has got my vote. It's even got Richard Wattis in it – can things get any better?

As well as the cast performing at the peak of their powers, the direction and set design are also very impressive. The film opens (great music, by the way) with a magnificent tracking shot that follows sinister milkman Victor Maddern into the heart of the Bilkington Research Establishment – setting the tone for some excellent black and white cinematography to come. Of special note are the sequences set in Vienna, which pay homage to the 1949 film *The Third Man* – all brooding shadows, wet cobbled streets and stylish zither music. Even when we arrive at the headquarters of STENCH, the high standards still hold up, with a passable Ken Adams-style underground base peopled by very Bondian women in tight black leather. Sadly, it all goes awry in the final 'conveyorbelt' sequence, with Gerald Thomas resolving our heroes' plight with not only a speeded-up sequence (the scourge of *Carry On* films), but a speeded-up sequence *in reverse*. Poor *Carry On* endings would often be the norm, but this is worse than most.

Verdict: Only the ending spoils what should have been a top score, which means *Spying* gets a near-perfect **4/5**.

10) Carry On Cleo (1964)

Cast: Kenneth Williams (Julius Caesar), Sid James (Mark Antony), Charles Hawtrey (Seneca), Joan Sims (Calpurnia), Jim Dale (Horsa), Kenneth Connor (Hengist Pod), Sheila Hancock (Senna Pod), Amanda Barrie (Cleopatra), Julie Stevens (Gloria), Victor Maddern (Sergeant Major), Jon Pertwee (Soothsayer), Brutus (Brian Oulton), Francis de Wolff (Agrippa), Michael Ward (Archimedes), Wanda Ventham (Beautiful Bidder), Tom Clegg (Sosages), Tanya Binning (Virginia), Peter Gilmore (Galley Master), David Davenport (Bilius), Ian Wilson (Messenger), Norman Mitchell (Heckler), Brian Rawlinson (Driver), Gertan Klauber (Markus), Warren Mitchell (Spencius), Peter Jesson (Companion), Michael Nightingale (Caveman), Judi Johnson (Gloria's Bridesmaid), Thelma Taylor (Seneca's Servant), Sally Douglas (Antony's Maiden), Peggy Ann Clifford (Willa Claudia), Mark Hardy (Guard), EVH Emmett (Narrator),

Christine Rodgers, Gloria Best, Virginia Tyler (Handmaidens), Gloria Johnson, Joanna Ford, Donna White, Jane Lumb, Vicki Smith (Vestal Virgins)

Crew: Director Gerald Thomas, Screenplay Talbot Rothwell (from an original idea by William Shakespeare), Producer Peter Rogers, Music Eric Rogers, Director of Photography Alan Hume, Editor Archie Ludski, Art Director Bert Davey, Assistant Director Peter Bolton, Unit Manager Donald Toms, Associate Producer Frank Bevis, Camera Operator Godfrey Godar, Continuity Olga Brook, Make-Up Geoff Rodway, Hairdresser Ann Fordyce, Costume Designer Julie Harris, Sound Recordists Bill Daniels & Gordon K McCallum, Sound Editor Christopher Lancaster (Anglo Amalgamated, November 1964, Eastmancolor, 92m, A/PG)

DVD: 2001 (Studio Canal, D038032)

Story: In Ancient Rome, Julius Caesar (Kenneth Williams) and Mark Antony (Sid James) vie for the attention of sultry Egyptian Queen Cleopatra (Amanda Barrie)...

Notable Lines: Kenneth Williams: 'My last immortal words are '*Veni, vedi, veci*' – I came, I saw, I conked out!' / Joan Sims: 'Seneca is well known throughout Rome as a truly great sage.' Charles Hawtrey: 'Yes, and I know my onions.' / Jim Dale: 'If anyone in there asks who we are, say we're eunuchs.' Kenneth Connor: 'Eh? Oh yeah, what have we got to lose?' / Sid James: 'What a carve up!' / Kenneth Williams: 'Where's me laurels? Oh, silly me, I've been resting on 'em!' / Sid James: 'They call her the Siren of the Nile.' Kenneth Williams: 'Oh, I hope she don't go off. I mean, they do tend to in those hot countries, don't they?' Sid James: 'You don't want to worry about that – she's got a deep frieze running all the way round the walls of the palace.' / Kenneth Connor: 'I'm trying to find a clean pitcher.' Kenneth Williams: 'Oh forget it. Try to remember you're in Egypt – they only have dirty pitchers here.' / Kenneth Williams: 'Infamy! Infamy! They've all got it in for me!' / Kenneth Williams: 'Tony!' Sid James: 'Julie!' and many, many more...

Key Scene: In a film overflowing with wonderful moments, it's hard to pick one. How about the running gag with Kenneth Williams trying to deliver the famous 'Friends, Romans...' speech only to be prompted 'Countrymen!' every time? Great stuff.

Observations: In the dream sequence showing Amanda Barrie getting out of the bath of asses' milk, she is clearly wearing knickers.

The film anachronistically has cavemen referring to a brontosaurus – both wildly predating the reign of Cleopatra (c. 69–30 BC).

All Dragged Up: Kenneth Connor and Jim Dale as vestal virgins.

Review: Perfect things – be they people, paintings or films – are difficult to analyse: they just *are. Cleo* is a perfect *Carry On* film – it just is. From the opening credits with their hilarious 'from an original idea by William Shakespeare' caption, to the hair-pulling marriage ceremony at the end, via Sid James' 'Blimus!' and Kenneth Williams' 'Infamy!' speech (quite possibly the most famous line in *Carry On* history, and rightfully so), the whole film screams classic at you. There is not one single scene, barely one single line, which is not squeezed dry for comedic value. The puns are excruciatingly bad, the delivery deadpan, the setting detailed and believable. Even the fluffs are perfect – Brian Oulton corpsing as Williams delivers his Churchillian rhetoric, or Williams himself stumbling over 'What say you?' during his first death scene.

The secret of this film's success, as has been noted by better people than me, is that the actors play it as if it's a contemporary comedy with togas. There's none of that *Jack* rubbish about being historically accurate. This is like a feature-length *Morecambe and Wise* play, only without the padding and the flat delivery of the guest star. The regulars are brilliant (even Kenneth Connor), Amanda Barrie is sultry and funny, Jon Pertwee is at his batty best, and we've even got gorgeous *Play School* presenter Julie Stevens in a fur bikini – I mean, what more could you people want? In fact, why are you reading this at all and not watching the film? Blimey, even Kenneth Williams liked it. ('Tuesday 12 May 1964… I got the script of *Carry On Cleo* today and I must say I think it is very funny.')

Verdict: I'm not allowed to give it a 6, so I'll have to settle for an historic **5/5**.

11) Carry On Cowboy (1965)

Cast: Jim Dale (Marshall P Knutt), Sid James (Johnny Finger/The Rumpo Kid), Kenneth Williams (Judge Burke), Joan Sims (Belle), Angela Douglas (Annie Oakley), Peter Butterworth (Doc), Charles Hawtrey (Big Heap), Bernard Bresslaw (Little Heap), Jon Pertwee (Sheriff Albert Earp), Davy Kaye (Josh the Undertaker), Percy Herbert (Charlie), Sydney Bromley (Sam Houston),

Edina Ronay (Dolores), Lionel Murton (Clerk), Simon Cain (Short), Peter Gilmore (Curly), Alan Gifford (Commissioner), Brian Rawlinson (Stage Coach Guard), Michael Nightingale (Bank Manager), Sally Douglas (Kitkata), Carl McFord (Mex), Garry Colleano (Slim), Arthur Lovegrove (Old Cowhand), Margaret Nolan (Miss Jones), Tom Clegg (Blacksmith), Brian Coburn (Trapper), Larry Cross (Perkins), Norman Stanley (Drunk), Hal Galili (Cowhand), Carmen Dene (Mexican Girl), Gloria West (Bridget), Lisa Thomas (Sally), Donna White (Jenny), Audrey Wilson (Jane), Vicki Smith (Polly), Andrea Allen (Minnie), George Mossman (Stage Coach Driver), Rider (Richard O'Brien), Eric Rogers (Pianist), The Ballet Montparnesse (Dancing Girls)

Crew: Director Gerald Thomas, Screenplay Talbot Rothwell, Producer Peter Rogers, Music Eric Rogers ('Carry On Cowboy' & 'This Is The Night For Love' – music Eric Rogers, lyrics Alan Rogers), Director of Photography Alan Hume, Editor Rod Keys, Art Director Bert Davey, Assistant Editor Jack Gardner, Assistant Director Peter Bolton, Unit Manager Ron Jackson, Camera Operator Godfrey Godar, Continuity Gladys Goldsmith, Make-Up Geoffrey Rodway, Hairdresser Stella Rivers, Costume Designer Cynthia Tingey, Sound Recordists Robert T MacPhee & Ken Barker, Sound Editor Jim Groom, Master of Horse Jeremy Taylor (Anglo Amalgamated, November 1965, Eastmancolor, 95m, A/PG)

DVD: 2001 (Studio Canal, D038034)

Story: Stodge City's Judge Burke (Kenneth Williams) wants a new Marshall to clean it up. Unfortunately he gets Jim Dale instead…

Notable Lines: Kenneth Williams: 'I thought I heard shots just now.' Peter Butterworth: 'Probably just a horse backfiring.' / Kenneth Williams: 'I am the Mayor.' Sid James: 'You'd better keep away from my horse – he ain't seen a mare for three weeks.' / Kenneth Williams: 'It ain't safe for decent folks to walk the streets at night. Why, I have to send the wife out for everything!' / Sid James: 'Once talked peace with the Sioux, but you can't trust 'em. One minute it was peace on, the next, peace off.' / Charles Hawtrey: 'I can't stand actors myself. Very peculiar lot.' / Kenneth Williams: 'My great-grandfather came over here in the *Mayflower*. He was the original Burke. Married into the Wright family and became a Wright Burke.' / Jim Dale: 'They got away with 40 cows.' Sid James: 'Bullocks.' Jim Dale: 'I know what I'm talking about.'

Key Scene: The cunning way that Jim Dale dispatches the baddies is a neat sequence that always makes me smile.

Observations: When George Mossman is hit by an arrow, he is clearly holding it to his chest before flicking it up. Sid James changes the population of Stodge City from '204' to '201' after he shoots down the three men at the start, but then it stays this way even after Jon Pertwee's character is killed.

Locations: Chobham Common, Surrey, and Black Park, Fulmer, Bucks.

Review: After the tremendous success of *Cleo* comes another assured historical romp. But *Cowboy* is subtly different to its immediate predecessor, because it harks back to the *Jack* notion of locating the story within a credible historical setting. Rather than having the cast look as if they're performing in an end-of-the-pier revue, in *Cowboy* the situations and setting are all played for real. The film works as drama as well as comedy – *Cowboy*, as Kenneth Williams recognised in his *Diaries*, is 'the first time a British Western has ever been done.' And done extremely well. All the location work is convincing (despite the English scenery) and the Indian attack on the stagecoach is an impressive piece of editing, managing to achieve its aims without recourse to yellowing old stock footage (another *Carry On* scourge). It may be the Pinewood backlot, but Stodge City is as believable a settlement as anything that a *bona fide* Hollywood Western produced.

Sid James manages to put in a solid performance that is convincingly naturalistic – he *is* the Rumpo Kid – and provides the core around which the other performers gravitate. Joan Sims, likewise, plays her role as the local Madam dead straight. It's left to Kenneth Williams' aged judge – a mass of nervous tics and scrunched face-pulling – and Jim Dale ('Draining, Sanitation and Garbage Disposal Engineer, First Class – with a certificate from Chipping Sodbury Technical College to prove it!') to provide the character parts. Dale is as clumsy and incompetent as he ever would be – if you like him, then this is the film for you. If you don't, best skip to *Screaming!* where his performance is significantly toned down.

It's not all laughs, though – there are several deaths on screen, and Jim Dale is almost strung from a tree at one point. But then this is a *Carry On* film, so we have a surfeit of corny visual gags (mostly of the equine variety) to prevent the material from becoming too grim: saddling your horse and riding it across the street, matching horses' hoofprints, even putting your horse to sleep at night in a bed. The *High Noon* in-joke at the end provides the icing on the cake.

The last word must go to Charles Hawtrey, whose Indian Chief Big Heap is a marvellous creation. From his first appearance, emerging from a tepee to the sound of a flushing toilet, his entire performance is charmingly offbeat. Blending Received Pronunciation with a naff 'Injun' patois ('Confidentially, Big Heap have heap big hangum-over'), this is quite possibly Hawtrey's most satisfying role ever – who else could deliver the line 'Oompa stickedy jumper! Bloody quick!' quite so wonderfully as he? Kenneth Williams, writing in his *Diaries* on 9 February 1966, said, 'It's got laughs, and pathos, some lovely people and ugly people. Mind you, it's an alarming thought that they'll never top this one.' But they almost did – with the very next film…

Verdict: For making a funnier Western than the Americans ever did, a ten-gallon **5/5**.

12) Carry On Screaming! (1966)

Cast: Harry H Corbett (Detective Sergeant Sidney Bung), Kenneth Williams (Dr Orlando Watt), Peter Butterworth (Detective Constable Slobotham), Jim Dale (Albert Potter), Fenella Fielding (Valeria Watt), Charles Hawtrey (Dan Dann), Joan Sims (Emily Bung), Bernard Bresslaw (Sockett), Angela Douglas (Doris Mann), Jon Pertwee (Dr Fettle), Tom Clegg (Oddbod), Billy Cornelius (Oddbod Junior), Norman Mitchell (Cabby), Michael Ward (Window Dresser), Frank Thornton (Mr Jones), Frank Forsyth (Desk Sergeant), Anthony Sagar (Policeman), Sally Douglas (Girl), Marianne Stone (Mrs Parker), Denis Blake (Rubbatiti)

Crew: Director Gerald Thomas, Screenplay Talbot

Rothwell, Producer Peter Rogers, Music Eric Rogers
('Carry on Screaming' by Myles Rudge & Ted Dick, sung
by 'Boz' [Raymond Burrell]), Director of Photography
Alan Hume, Editor Rod Keys, Art Director Bert Davey,
Assistant Director Peter Bolton, Unit Manager Ron
Jackson, Associate Producer Frank Bevis, Camera
Operator Godfrey Godar, Continuity Penny Daniels,
Make-Up Geoff Rodway, Hairdresser Stella Rivers,
Costume Designer Emma Selby-Walker, Sound
Recordists CC Stevens & Ken Barker, Sound Editor
Arthur Ridout (Anglo Amalgamated, August 1966,
Eastmancolor, 97m, A/PG)

DVD: 2001 (Studio Canal, D038039)

Story: When young ladies start disappearing in the woods,
Detective Bung (Harry H Corbett) suspects all is not as it
should be at the sinister Bide-A-Wee Rest Home...

Notable Lines: Harry H Corbett: 'Did you get a description?' Peter Butterworth: 'Naturally. It's a Miss Doris Mann;
aged about 20, medium height, average hair colour, ordinary
eyes, wearing clothes.' / Peter Butterworth: 'It was something unspeakable.' Harry H Corbett: 'Unspeakable?' Peter
Butterworth: 'Yes, it never said a word.' / Harry H Corbett:
'What's the name of this road, Slobotham?' Peter
Butterworth: 'Avery Avenue.' Harry H Corbett: 'Then we
must explore Avery Avenue.' / Harry H Corbett: 'Your name
please?' Kenneth Williams: 'Dr Watt.' Peter Butterworth: 'Dr
who?' Kenneth Williams: 'Watt. Who is my uncle.' / Fenella
Fielding: 'Why don't we do what they did to your friend
Dracula – drive a spike through his heart.' Kenneth Williams:
'No, I don't really feel like driving tonight.' / Kenneth
Williams: 'Frying tonight!' and many more...

Key Scene: For my money, it's got to be the scene when Harry H Corbett visits the drop-dead gorgeous Fenella Fielding. She asks if he minds her smoking, and then she proceeds to lie back and smoulder seductively, wreathed in clouds of smoke!

Observations: Billy Cornelius (Oddbod Junior) falls over the rubble after he walks through the wall. The 'snake in the bed' joke is stolen from *What a Carve Up!* (1962) with Sid James and Kenneth Connor.

All Dragged Up: Peter Butterworth in wig and corset as the killer's bait.

Location: Windsor, Berks, and Fulmer, Bucks.

Review: Whatever they put in the water when they made *Cowboy* was still having its effect when the team produced this utterly charming Hammer Horror spoof. There really isn't much to say about this classic film, except that it is pretty near faultless in every department. Visually sumptuous, wittily scripted and brought to life by a team of dedicated professionals. What can one say except 'Encore!'

The title music is in *Cowboy* mode, with an amusing Presley-style ballad in which – rather snazzily – the titles shiver whenever the word 'Screaming' is sung. There's strong, scary music throughout the film (as well as sly references to TV shows *Z Cars* and *Steptoe and Son*), backing up the notion that, like *Cowboy*, the threat to our heroes is all too real. The 'jokes per minute' quota is on overdrive and there's some hysterical fast patter of the music-hall kind (for example, the 'whereabouts' routine). Picking out individual cast members is invidious, but special mention must go to Harry H Corbett in his only *Carry On* appearance. He is excellent in a role surely intended for Sid James (the character's name is Sidney after all) and milks the hoary old jokes as only a man of his comedy talents can. Peter Butterworth is also on top form as the other half of the double act. As to the others, well, Fenella Fielding is as gorgeous as ever – a cross between Morticia Addams and Vampira from *Plan 9 from Outer Space* – while Kenneth Williams delivers his terrible puns with enthusiasm. 'Fangs aren't what they used to be' indeed!

Gerald Thomas' direction is effective, following shot for shot the standard conventions of the horror genre, complete with swirling fog, dark woods and creepy sound effects. The visual effects are impressive too, such as when Kenneth Williams' head fades away, leaving his clothing still visible, or the finger that grows into a life-size monster (very similar to a scene in the 1972 Peter Cushing horror film, *The Creeping Flesh*). The idea of attaching electrodes to Williams' protuberant ears is inspired.

Verdict: I would have to be a zombie not to give this a richly deserved **5/5**.

13) (Carry On) Don't Lose Your Head (1966)

Cast: Sid James (Sir Rodney Ffing/The Black Fingernail), Jim Dale (Lord Darcy de Pue), Kenneth Williams (Citizen Camembert), Charles Hawtrey (Duc de Pommfrit), Joan Sims (Desirée Dubarry), Peter Butterworth (Citizen Bidet), Dany Robin (Jacqueline), Peter Gilmore (Robespierre), Michael Ward (Henri), Marianne Stone (Landlady), Leon Greene (Malabonce), Hugh Futcher (Guard), Richard Shaw (Captain), David

Davenport (Sergeant), Jennifer Clulow (First Lady), Valerie Van Ost (Second Lady), Jacqueline Pearce (Third Lady), Nikki Van Der Zyl (Messenger), Julian Orchard (Rake), Joan Ingram (Bald Dowager), Elspeth March (Lady Binder), Michael Nightingale (Locket Man), Diana MacNamara (Princess Stephanie), Ronnie Brody (Little Man), Billy Cornelius (Soldier), Patrick Allen (Narrator), Monica Dietrich, Anna Willoughby, Penny Keen, June Cooper, Christine Pryor, Karen Young (Girls)

Crew: Director Gerald Thomas, Screenplay Talbot Rothwell, Producer Peter Rogers, Music Eric Rogers ('Don't Lose Your Head' by Bill Martin & Phil Coulter, executed by The Michael Sammes Singers), Director of Photography Alan Hume, Editor Rod Keys, Art Director Lionel Couch, Assistant Director Jack Causey, Production Manager Jack Swinburne, Camera Operator Jimmy Devis, Continuity Rita Davison, Make-Up Geoffrey Rodway, Hairdresser Stella Rivers, Costume Designer Emma Selby-Walker, Sound Recordists Dudley Messenger & Ken Barker, Sound Editor Wally Nelson, Master of Horse Jeremy Taylor, Choreographer Terry Gilbert (Rank, December 1966, Eastmancolor, 90m, A/PG)

DVD: 2003 (Carlton, 3711503393, SE)

Story: Sir Rodney Ffing (Sid James) sets out to rescue the beleaguered aristocrats of France under the guise of The Black Fingernail...

Notable Lines: Peter Gilmore: 'It seems that the English have struck again.' Kenneth Williams: 'Yes, Citizen Robespierre, but then they say it's the one thing the English are good at – striking.' / Kenneth Williams: 'I've got it! I've got it!' Joan Sims: 'Well, you didn't get it off me.' / Kenneth Williams: 'You must be circumspect.' Peter Butterworth: 'Oh I was, sir, when I was a baby.' / Kenneth Williams: 'As the injured party, I have the choice of swords or pistols.' Sid James: 'Oh, we won't quarrel over that. You have the swords, I'll have the pistols.' Kenneth Williams: 'Do not jest, sir – believe me, I am deadly earnest.' Sid James: 'And I'm living Rodney, and I'm going to stay that way.'

Key Scene: The 'pistols at dawn' duel. Obviously.

Observations: The changeover to Rank necessitated that the 'Carry On' prefix be dropped for this film and the next. However, when the films performed disappointingly at the box office, the familiar addition was tacked on to posters and publicity material, but not to the film print itself. I have therefore included the prefix in parenthesis only.

All Dragged Up: Sid James as an aristocratic lady.

Locations: Black Park, Bucks; Waddesdon Manor, Waddesdon, Bucks; Clandon Park, West Clandon, Guildford, Surrey; Cliveden, Bucks.

Review: Following a trend that began with *Cowboy*, the film opens with a song – this time a gloriously tasteless cross between the tune of Rolf Harris' 'Two Little Boys' and the lyrics of 'Always Look on the Bright Side of Life' from *Monty Python's Life of Brian*. After Raymond Allen's stirring narration – always the sign of a classic – we get a prolonged beheading sequence that, although bloodless, sets up the rather grim premise of this French Revolution spoof. Then it's straight into the action with Sid James as a camp dandy with a lisp, Jim Dale dusting off his suave persona from *Spying*, and Kenneth Williams as the incompetent ruler à la *Cleo*. Add to the mix Joan Sims in full 'common tart' mode and Peter Butterworth as a typically dopey henchman, and all the film needs is an excellent script to raise it to classic status.

It gets it. Talbot Rothwell is on absolute top form here. Flushed with success from his previous three historicals, and firing on all cylinders, he produces a joke-filled screenplay that is chock-full of choice witticisms, coarse put-downs and silly visual gags. There's much play on the name 'Ffing' (pronounced 'Effing'), Peter Butterworth is told to 'get it out' and lines such as 'you've always had magnificent balls' are delivered with unabashed solemnity. Add the magnificent production values, lush location filming and an impressive extended sword fight with much comic business and you have a worthy contender for the 'Top 5' *Carry On* films.

There's very little to criticise here, but I will mention a few niggles. The main one is Charles Hawtrey, who comes across as rather unsympathetic. We first see him laughing uproariously at a volume of the Marquis de Sade, and he continues through the narrative as a womanising braggart with few redeeming features. He is, of course, funny, but his character is less appealing than normal. There are a few duff jokes (the wigs blown onto the wrong people doesn't really work) and the ending's rather flat, but these are minor points. Peter Gilmore's 'Mon blooming dieu!', Kenneth Williams' ad libbed 'Mind me hat!' to Peter Butterworth as they jostle for place in the stagecoach, Williams' resurrection of his 'Sheriff' character from *Cowboy*, the Baroque version of The Beatles' 'She Loves Me'; these things (and more) far outweigh any small dissatisfaction. There's also a lot of talking straight to the camera, in particular the fine first scene between Sid James and Dany Robin, which consists almost solely of asides to the audience, and therefore it's fair to say that this is the most pantomimic of all the *Carry Ons* – and one of the highest compliments I could pay. Not for nothing was it released at Christmas.

Verdict: For executing a *Boy's Own* adventure story with verve, good humour and the maximum of corny jokes, it has to get **5/5**. *Tres bien!*

14) (Carry On) Follow That Camel (1967)

Cast: Phil Silvers (Sergeant Ernie Nocker), Jim Dale (Bertram Oliphant 'BO' West), Peter Butterworth (Simpson), Kenneth Williams (Commandant Burger), Charles Hawtrey (Captain Le Pice), Joan Sims (Zig-Zag), Angela Douglas (Lady Jane Ponsonby), Anita Harris (Corktip), Bernard Bresslaw (Sheikh Abdul Abulbul), John Bluthal (Corporal Clotski), William Mervyn (Sir Cyril Ponsonby), Peter Gilmore (Captain Bagshaw), Edmund Pegge (Bowler), Julian Holloway (Ticket Collector), David Glover (Hotel Manager), Larry Taylor (Riff), William Hurndell (Raff), Vincent Ball (Ship's Officer), Julian Orchard (Doctor), Peter Jesson (Lawrence), Gertan Klauber (Spiv), Michael Nightingale (Butler), Richard Montez, Frank Singuineau, Simon Cain (Riffs at Abdul's Tent), Harold Kasket (Hotel Gentleman), Carol Sloan, Gina Gianelli, Dominique Don, Anne Scott, Patsy Snell, Zorenah Osborne, Margot Maxine, Sally Douglas, Angie Grant, Gina Warwick, Karen Young, Helga Jones (Harem Girls)

Crew: Director Gerald Thomas, Screenplay Talbot Rothwell, Producer Peter Rogers, Music Eric Rogers, Director of Photography Alan Hume, Editor Alfred Roome, Art Director Alex Vetchinsky, Assistant Editor Jack Gardner, Assistant Director David Bracknell, Production Manager Jack Swinburne, Camera Operator Alan Hall, Continuity Joy Mercer, Make-Up Geoffrey Rodway, Hairdresser Stella Rivers, Costume Designer Emma Selby-Walker, Sound Recordists Dudley Messenger & Ken Barker, Dubbing Editor Wally Nelson, Location Manager Terry Clegg (Rank, September 1967, Eastmancolor, 95m, A/PG)

DVD: 2003 (Carlton, 3711503423, SE)

Story: England, 1906. 'BO' West (Jim Dale) and his manservant Simpson (Peter Butterworth) join the Foreign Legion, only to face the terrifying Sheikh Abdul Abulbul (Bernard Bresslaw) and his band of bloodthirsty Bedouins…

Notable Lines: Bernard Bresslaw: 'Peace on you.' Phil Silvers: 'And peace on you too.' / Kenneth Williams: 'These hot-blooded Arabs – once they get you amongst the sand dunes, ooh!' Angela Douglas: 'Oh do tell me, what do they do?' Kenneth Williams: 'Oh, I cannot tell you. But there's an old Arab saying: "There's many a good fiddle played on an old dune."' / Phil Silvers: 'The Pill? What do you suppose they use that for?' Kenneth Williams: 'I can't conceive.'

Key Scene: A tie between the surreal sequence of the straggling Legionaires singing 'Oh, I do like to be beside the seaside!' and Hawtrey's endearing sandcastle competition. Both have a delightfully childish appeal.

MARK CAMPBELL

Observations: Once again, the film does not contain the 'Carry On' prefix (see *Don't Lose Your Head*).

All Dragged Up: Peter Butterworth as Lady Jane Ponsonby.

Locations: Camber Sands and Rye, East Sussex.

Review: It's easy to view this film as merely a dry run for the superior *Carry On... Up the Khyber*, released the following year. But while the basic setting and period are similar, *Follow That Camel* feels quite different thanks to its unique visual look. For instance, there are many sequences that could have come straight from a silent film, such as Peter Butterworth trying to escape the clutches of Bernard Bresslaw, played out in silhouette through the Sheikh's tent. The location filming is extremely effective too, making this entry one of the most cinematically satisfying *Carry On*s. Clever photography ensures that the windswept Camber Sands never look anything less than a baking hot Egyptian desert.

Of course, the film's main claim to fame is the odd – but ultimately successful – casting of American comedian Phil Silvers in a key role (replacing the ill Sid James). His Vaudeville style of comic banter matches that of the regular team members' music hall delivery to such an extent that you forget any difference in accent. Of the regulars, Jim Dale and Peter Butterworth stand out for their nicely understated performances, especially the former, who has presumably discovered that to be funny 'less is more'. Kenneth Williams, clearly relishing the chance to do something a bit different, makes the most of his sadistic German Commandant, while an ever-reliable Charles Hawtrey minces around as his second-incommand. Bernard Bresslaw is excellent as the villain, a role he would repeat verbatim for *Khyber*. Sadly, the female members of the team are not so well treated: Joan Sims has hardly any lines, while Anita Harris (too svelte for a belly dancer, surely) makes as little impression as Angela Douglas, who here plays a naïve English girl abused by a succession of dirty old men – a far cry from the strong character she had played in *Cowboy*. (The scenes of implied rape – 'What an odd way to check my porthole!' – are horribly misogynistic.)

Follow That Camel is a good example of a historical *Carry On*, but not the best. Whether it's the absence of Sid James or the over-familiarity of the genre (this was the fifth historical in a row), it's impossible to say. At times the starkness of its material – a suicide in the first few minutes, men staked out in the sand for days on end, a climactic massacre – resembles more a big-screen *Ripping Yarns* tale than a *Carry On* outing. That said, any film that has someone hitting explosive coconuts over a wall with a cricket bat must have something going for it.

Verdict: I'm going to give it **4/5** because I think it lacks that extra-special something.

15) Carry On Doctor (1967)

Cast: Frankie Howerd (Francis Bigger), Jim Dale (Dr Jim Kilmore), Kenneth Williams (Dr Kenneth Tinkle), Sid James (Charlie Roper), Charles Hawtrey (Mr Barron), Hattie Jacques (Matron Lavinia), Peter Butterworth (Mr Smith), Bernard Bresslaw (Ken Biddle), Joan Sims (Chloe Gibson), Barbara Windsor (Nurse Sandra May), Anita Harris (Nurse Clarke), June Jago (Sister Hoggett), Dilys Laye (Mavis), Peter Gilmore (Henry), Harry Locke

(Sam), Gwendolyn Watts (Mrs Barron), Derek Francis (Sir Edmund Burke), Dandy Nichols (Mrs Roper), Derek Guyler (Surgeon Hardcastle), Julian Orchard (Fred), Marianne Stone (Mum), Stephen Garlick (Boy), Bart Allison (Granddad), Peter Jones (Chaplain), Jean St Clair (Mrs Smith), Valerie Van Ost (Nurse Parkin), Brian Wilde (Plastic Sheet Man), Lucy Griffiths, Pat Coombs (Patients), Gertan Klauber (Wash Orderly), Simon Cain (Tea Orderly), Julian Holloway (Simmons), Jenny White (Nurse in Bath), Helen Ford, Jane Murdoch (Nurses), Gordon Rollings (Night Porter), Cheryl Molineaux (Caffin Ward Nurse), Alexandra Dane (Female Instructor), Ned Caralius (Mr Wrigley), Patrick Allen (Narrator)

Crew: Director Gerald Thomas, Screenplay Talbot Rothwell, Producer Peter Rogers, Music Eric Rogers, Director of Photography Alan Hume, Editor Alfred Roome, Art Director Cedric Dawes, Assistant Editor Jack Gardner, Assistant Director Terry Clegg, Production Manager Jack Swinburne, Camera Operator Jim Bawden, Continuity Joy Mercer, Make-Up Geoffrey Rodway, Hairdresser Stella Rivers, Costume Designer Yvonne Caffin, Sound Recordists Dudley Messenger & Ken Barker, Dubbing Editor David Campling, Title Sketches by 'Larry' (Rank, December 1967, Eastmancolor, 94m, A/PG)

Alternatively: 'Nurse Carries On Again' or 'Death of a Daffodil' or 'Life Is a Four-Letter Ward' or 'A Bedpanarama of Hospital Life'

DVD: 2003 (Carlton, 3711503373, SE)

Story: After injuring his back, faith healer Francis Bigger (Frankie Howerd) is admitted to a county hospital where he sees what life is *really* like in the NHS...

Notable Lines: Frankie Howerd: 'The triumph of mind over matter! What is mind? No matter. What is matter? Never mind.' / Anita Harris: 'Matron doesn't approve of banging in the ward.' / Bernard Bresslaw: 'I dreamt about you last night.' Anita Harris: 'Did you?' Bernard Bresslaw: 'No, you wouldn't let me.' / Kenneth Williams: 'It's an enigma. That's what it is, Matron, an enigma.' Sid James: 'I am not having another one of those!' / Kenneth Williams: 'Slight bruising, certainly. No bleeding – good.' Frankie Howerd: 'Just like the service round here.' / Barbara Windsor: 'Oh, what a lovely looking pear!' / Hattie Jacques: 'Young chickens may be soft and tender, but the older birds have more on them.' Kenneth Williams: 'True – and take a lot more stuffing.' / Kenneth Williams: 'You may not realise it, but I was once a weak man.' Hattie Jacques: 'Once a week's enough for any man.'

Key Scene: I love the moment when Hattie Jacques looks doe-eyed at Kenneth Williams and thinks 'I love you!', while the object of her affection looks in the mirror and thinks exactly the same thing – about himself. (What makes this so poignant is that Williams did the same thing in real life – according to his *Diaries*, he would often stand in front of his mirror and think to himself how gorgeous he looked.)

Observations: There's a star-shaped wipe from one scene to the next – not a device that had ever been used before, and then only once in this film. Just after Kenneth Williams promises to give Sid James an ice bath, part of the camera mechanism comes into view at the bottom of the picture. Caffin Ward is named after costume designer Yvonne Caffin, and in homage to the successful *Doctor...* film series, a portrait of James Robertson Justice hangs in the reception of the hospital.

All Dragged Up: Bernard Bresslaw as a nurse.

Locations: Maidenhead Town Hall, Berks.

Review: Almost a decade after *Carry On Nurse* comes this belated sequel, which is nothing more than a retread of the first film, albeit in colour (the first alternative title, 'Nurse Carries On Again' says it all). Once again it details the day-to-day happenings of a male hospital ward, and once again it ends with a morbid operating room scene. There's the added novelty of a female ward across the corridor, and as Barbara Windsor appears (after a five-film gap, and looking better in her nurse's uniform than out of it), breast gags replace penis gags, but otherwise nothing else has changed. In a delightfully self-referential moment, Frankie Howerd even refers to the ending of *Nurse* when he's approached by a nurse with a daffodil and squawks, 'Oh no you don't – I saw that film!'

The trouble is that, like the first film, *Doctor* is hopelessly arthritic. The patients spend most of their time in bed (at least Sid James had a good reason – he was recuperating from a heart attack) and the structure of the film is all over the place. For instance, Barbara Windsor gets a big introduction as Kenneth Williams' obsessive stalker, but then disappears halfway through. The filmmakers also err in giving Bernard Bresslaw a large comedy part when he doesn't have the necessary skills for it – witness his embarrassing high-pitched shouting, silly walk and rolling

eyes. Worst scene has to be when Howerd is marrying
Joan Sims, despite Peter Jones' valiant efforts as the chaplain. The scene has so much promise and yet it just trickles
along without so much as a punchline.

That said, there are plenty of good things on offer.
Charles Hawtrey is compelling as the strange little man
with the phantom pregnancy, Frankie Howerd gives the
limp narrative much needed 'oomph', and Hattie Jacques'
unrequited love for Kenneth Williams is a great notion
that would see several more outings in later films. Joan
Sims displays rare virtuosity in her role as dowdy, hard-of-
hearing wife to Francis Bigger – a world away from the
tarts and domineering wives/mothers she usually portrays.
The production standards are generally good, with the big
set piece when Jim Dale climbs onto the roof to 'rescue'
Barbara Windsor particularly well staged, thanks to near
faultless back projection and a convincing studio set.

Verdict: Kenneth Williams in his *Diaries* (10 August
1967) says, 'a v. good vehicle for Frankie Howerd but all
the other parts are lousy.' He's not wrong. **3/5**.

16) Carry On... Up the Khyber (1968)

Cast: Sid James (Sir Sidney Ruff-Diamond), Kenneth
Williams (Rhandi Lal, Khasi of Kalabar), Charles Hawtrey
(Private Widdle), Joan Sims (Lady Joan Ruff-Diamond),
Roy Castle (Captain Keene), Bernard Bresslaw (Bunghit
Din), Terry Scott (Sergeant-Major MacNutt), Peter
Butterworth (Brother Belcher), Angela Douglas (Princess
Jelhi), Julian Holloway (Major Shorthouse), Cardew
Robinson (The Fakir), Peter Gilmore (Ginger Hale),
Leon Thau (Stinghi), Michael Mellinger (Chindi),
Alexandra Dane (Busti), Dominique Don (Belcher's Tart),

Derek Sydney (Major Domo), David Spenser (Bunghit's Servant), Johnny Briggs (Sporran Soldier), Simon Cain (Bagpipe Soldier), Steven Scott (Guard Burpa), Larry Taylor (Door Burpa), Patrick Westwood (Crowd Burpa), John Hallam (Rooftop Burpa), Wanda Ventham, Liz Gold, Vicki Woolf, Anne Scott, Barbara Evans, Lisa Noble, Eve Eden, Tamsin MacDonald, Katherina Holden (Khasi's Wives), Valerie Leon, Carmen Dene, June Cooper, Josephine Blain, Karen Young, Angie Grant, Vicki Murden, Sue Vaughan (Harem Girls), Patrick Allen (Narrator)

Crew: Director Gerald Thomas, Screenplay Talbot Rothwell, Producer Peter Rogers, Music Eric Rogers, Director of Photography (Pinewood) Ernest Steward, Director of Photography (Snowdonia) HAR Thompson, Editor Alfred Roome, Art Director Alex Vetchinsky, Assistant Editor Jack Gardner, Assistant Director Peter Weingreen, Production Manager Jack Swinburne, Camera Operator (Pinewood) James Bawden, Camera Operator (Snowdonia) Neil Binney, Continuity Yvonne Richards, Make-Up Geoffrey Rodway, Hairdresser Stella Rivers, Costume Designer Emma Selby-Walker, Sound Recordists Robert T MacPhee & Ken Barker, Dubbing Editor Colin Miller, Title Sketches by 'Larry' (Rank, September 1968, Eastmancolor, 88m, A/PG)

Alternatively: 'The British Position in India'

DVD: 2003 (Canal, 3711503443, SE)

Story: India, 1895, and the Third Foot and Mouth Regiment are charged with guarding the Khyber Pass from the savage Burpas. But the regiment harbours a terrible secret that might just lead to its downfall...

Notable Lines: Sid James: 'I wouldn't trust him an inch.'
Joan Sims: 'Oh, neither would I.' Sid James: 'I didn't mean
that.' / Sid James: 'Well played, Philip! He'll go far, that boy
– if he makes the right marriage.' / Kenneth Williams:
'May the benevolence of the God Shiva bring blessing on
your home.' Sid James: 'And on yours.' Kenneth Williams:
'And may his wisdom bring success in all your undertak-
ings.' Sid James: 'And in yours.' Kenneth Williams: 'And
may his radiance light up your life.' Sid James: 'And up
yours.' / Roy Castle (seeing the harem girls): 'It must be a
trap.' Charles Hawtrey: 'Let's walk into it.' / Kenneth
Williams: 'They will die the death of a thousand cuts.'
Angela Douglas: 'Oh, that's horrible.' Kenneth Williams:
'Nonsense, child, the British are used to cuts.' / Peter
Butterworth: 'Charming! Join the army and see the next
world.' / Joan Sims: 'You haven't mentioned the dress.'
Kenneth Williams: 'Sari.' Joan Sims: 'Oh, there's no need to
apologise.' / Bernard Bresslaw: 'Fakir! Off!' / Sid James: '…
I therefore close your most respectable servant, Sidney
Ruff-Diamond, KCB, OBE, AC/DC, BBC, ITV, available
for private parties.' / Peter Butterworth: 'I've never ridden
in carts pulled by cows before.' Roy Castle: 'Bullocks.'
Peter Butterworth: 'No I haven't, honestly.' / Roy Castle:
'Fire at will.' Peter Butterworth: 'Poor old Will – why do
they always fire at him?' / Sid James: 'Under a flag of truce,
eh? I wonder what that means?' Julian Holloway: 'Well, sir,
it's a piece of white material stuck to a pole.' / Bernard
Bresslaw: 'It is a typical exhibition of the British phlegm.'
Kenneth Williams: 'I spit on their British phlegm!' /
Bernard Bresslaw: 'That will teach them to ban turbans on
the buses!'

Key Scene: The famous dinner scene as the Burpas bring
the room down around their ears has to be the one, but

with the proviso that it would be much better if Peter Butterworth wasn't in it – his overreactions spoil the British 'stiff upper lip' purity of everyone ignoring the destruction.

Observations: This is the only film to list the characters' names in the titles. The apple in the disembodied Fakir's mouth vanishes between shots. During the attack on the British Embassy, a bottle of wine explodes onto the camera lens.

All Dragged Up: Roy Castle, Peter Butterworth, Charles Hawtrey and Terry Scott as belly dancers.

Locations: Snowdonia, North Wales; Pinewood administration building.

Review: In a nutshell, *Khyber* is a work of genius. From the introductory stock footage to the final shot of the fluttering Union Jack with the slogan 'I'm Backing Britain', it's hard to think of 90 minutes of your time better spent. Built on the foundation of *Follow That Camel* and supported by the professionalism of *Cleo, Cowboy* and *Screaming, Carry On... Up the Khyber* has rightfully passed into the realm of cinema history as *the* archetypal *Carry On* film. One of Talbot Rothwell's most freewheeling and inventive scripts, it delightfully mocks British colonialism of the Victorian era, while at the same time celebrating the whole notion of 'Britishness' and inviting us to laugh at our peculiar quirks and foibles.

Kenneth Williams is absolutely wonderful, in arguably his best role. He brings a manic despotism to the part of the Khasi, which makes his occasional out-of-character lapses ('Oh, how many more times!') all the more exqui-

site. Note his audacious comic pause when he delivers the
line: 'flashing his great big... bayonet at me!' Charles
Hawtrey gets his most memorable role too, as the effemi-
nate Private ('It keeps my dangler warm!') Widdle. Sid
James, always having Tiffin, is at his most confident, while
the likes of Terry Scott, Peter Butterworth and Julian
Holloway provide solid backing. Playing to his strengths,
Bernard Bresslaw delivers another towering performance
of villainy (in a role lifted straight from *Follow That Camel*).

There are many fine touches. A sign outside the British
residency declares, 'No Hawkers, No Circulars, No
Fakirs', while a notice on the Khyber Pass reads simply,
'Please shut the gate'. The Fakir's tricks are a reminder of
the simple pleasures of silent film (Cardew Robinson
making his only appearance in the series) and even the
speeded-up fight sequence is somehow appropriate – it's
as if the filmmakers had so much stuff to pour in, they had
to speed up the action to accommodate it all, *Green Wing*
style. And there are some moments of satire that wouldn't
be out of place in *Airplane!*, such as when Hawtrey tells his
mate Ginger that he's going to snuff it ('Well, he said be
honest!') and the 'white flag' misunderstanding (see
above), which culminates in Holloway's seemingly ad
libbed exclamation, 'Oh... fudge!'

Like many of the best *Carry On*s, the grim nature of the
storyline adds bite to the humour. The massacre of the
British soldiers, lying there with spears and lances stuck in
them, is offset by Terry Scott's remark about cocktail
sticks, and the physical resemblance of the Burpas ('the
greatest fighters in all Afghanistan') to the Taliban adds
piquancy to the whole brew. In the midst of the climactic
fight scene, a Burpa says to a British soldier, 'Do you come
here often?' as they tussle in front of the camera. It's a
lovely moment in a film brimming with lovely moments.

Verdict: How could I give this anything other than a pukka **5/5**?

17) Carry On Camping (1969)

Cast: Sid James (Sid Boggle), Kenneth Williams (Dr Kenneth Soaper), Joan Sims (Joan Fussey), Charles Hawtrey (Charlie Muggins), Terry Scott (Peter Potter), Bernard Bresslaw (Bernie Lugg), Barbara Windsor (Babs), Hattie Jacques (Miss Haggard), Dilys Laye (Anthea Meeks), Peter Butterworth (Josh Fiddler), Julian Holloway (Jim Tanner), Betty Marsden (Harriet Potter), Trisha Noble (Sally), Amelia Bayntun (Mrs Fussey), Valerie Leon (Store Assistant), Brian Oulton (Store Manager), Derek Francis (Farmer), Patricia Franklin (Farmer's Daughter), Michael Nightingale (Man in Cinema), Sandra Caron (Fanny), George Moon (Scrawny Man), Valerie Shute (Pat), Elizabeth Knight (Jane), Georgina Moon (Joy), Vivien Lloyd (Verna), Jennifer Pyle (Hilda), Lesley Duff (Norma), Jackie Poole (Betty), Anna Karen (Hefty Girl), Sally Kemp (Girl with Cow), Peter Cockburn (Commentator), Gilly Grant (Sally G-String), Michael Low, Mike Lucas (Lusty Youths)

Crew: Director Gerald Thomas, Screenplay Talbot Rothwell, Producer Peter Rogers, Music Eric Rogers, Director of Photography Ernest Steward, Editor Alfred Roome, Art Director Lionel Couch, Assistant Editor Jack Gardner, Assistant Director Jack Causey, Production Manager Jack Swinburne, Camera Operator James Bawden, Continuity Doreen Dernley, Make-Up Geoffrey Rodway, Hairdresser Stella Rivers, Costume Designer Yvonne Caffin, Sound Recordists Bill Daniels & Ken Barker, Dubbing Editor Colin Miller, Title

Sketches by 'Larry' (Rank, February 1969, Eastmancolor, 88m, A/PG)

Alternatively: 'Let Sleeping Bags Lie'

DVD: 2003 (Carlton, 3711504463, SE)

Story: Various people go camping. And that's it.

Notable Lines: Joan Sims: 'I suppose you'd rather we sat here all stark naked.' Sid James: 'Wouldn't bother me.' Joan Sims: 'It would if your ice lolly fell in your lap.' / Charles Hawtrey: 'Oh, I've always been interested in camping.' / Charles Hawtrey: 'What's a nice girl like you doing with an old cow?' Sally Kemp: 'I'm taking her to the bull.' Charles Hawtrey: 'To the bull, oh – couldn't your father do that?' Sally Kemp: 'No, it has to be the bull.' / Charles Hawtrey (referring to Valerie Leon): 'Do you know, she's been showing me how to stick the pole up.'

Key Scene: The sequence of Charles Hawtrey, Terry Scott and Betty Marsden attempting to get undressed in the confines of their tiny tent is a brilliant piece of slapstick.

Observations: Because the film was shot in wintry conditions, the campsite mud was painted green to resemble grass (although it's impossible to see). Hattie Jacques mentions that she used to be a Matron in a hospital, an in-joke to her *Doctor* character.

Locations: Maidenhead, Berks; Pinewood Green, Bucks; Pinewood Studios' orchard (campsite); Juniper Cottages, Farnham Royal, Bucks (campsite entrance).

Review: This is always considered one of the most popular *Carry On* films, but watching it in the cold light of day it's hard to see what all the fuss is about. To most, it sticks in the mind for two reasons – Barbara Windsor. The scene in which she thrusts her chest out and her bra twangs off into the air is undoubtedly a good moment – but one scene does not a classic make, and although there are plenty of other good bits, the film as a whole is curiously unsatisfying.

Let's have a look at the good points first though (and no, I'm not talking about Barbara Windsor). For a start, the various actors give typically fine performances, with Terry Scott particularly amusing as the downtrodden husband to the irritating Betty Marsden. Whether he's being head-butted over a hedge by a bull (a cleverly edited sequence avoiding the need actually to see the animal), shot in the bum with pellets, or sharing his tent with the over-familiar Charles Hawtrey, he maintains a convincingly world-weary expression throughout. Sid James is, well, Sid James, and as such is fine, although he's now looking rather long in the tooth to be 'one of the lads'. Joan Sims and Dilys Laye perform their minor roles with efficiency, while Kenneth Williams makes the most of an under-written part. Charles Hawtrey seems to be acting in his own little film, so rarely does he come into contact with any of the other characters, and it seems quite reasonable when he goes off with the gang of hippies at the end. Bresslaw is just there to fill up the picture and poor Hattie Jacques looks somewhat marooned, away from the clinical corridors of a hospital or school. But Peter Butterworth excels as the money-grabbing Josh Fiddler, eager to squeeze that extra pound off the unwary campers.

On the downside, the storyline – such as it is – is unwarrantably lazy. The nudist film advertises Paradise

Camp Site, but when Sid's gang turns up no explanation is given for why it's suddenly *not* a nudist camp (other than it's just the wrong one, which is a bit lame). Then there's that weird sequence set in Steadfast Abbey that has no plot function at all. And it's always a giveaway when the only way to end a *Carry On* is by introducing a hitherto unmentioned element to provide a tacked-on conclusion. In this case it's a psychedelic pop band called The Flowerbuds who arrive in the adjacent field to hold an all-night rave. All differences are forgotten in the light of this dangerous new menace, and the campers team up to drive these young anarchists away – by threading rope through their bead necklaces and pulling them along with a tractor. Hmm.

The film also features one of the more unsavoury *Carry On* philosophies – namely, that a middle-aged henpecked husband can suddenly become a real man by having sex with a teenage girl. In fact, the lingering emphasis on the nubile pupils of Chayste Place smacks of voyeurism, and certainly the screen time devoted to young girls fighting, exercising and showering suggests more than an element of the 'dirty mac brigade'. There's a grey area between humorous sauciness and plain titillation, and I think *Camping* just crosses the line.

Verdict: For not being as good as everyone says, an average **3/5**.

18) Carry On Again Doctor (1969)

Cast: Jim Dale (Dr James Nookey), Kenneth Williams (Dr Frederick Carver), Sid James (Dr Gladstone Screwer), Charles Hawtrey (Dr Ernest Stoppidge), Joan Sims (Ellen Moore), Barbara Windsor (Goldie Locks/Maude

Boggins), Hattie Jacques (Matron), Pat Coombs (New Matron), Patsy Rowlands (Miss Fosdick), Peter Butterworth (Uncomfortable Patient), Wilfrid Brambell (Mr Pullen), Peter Gilmore (Henry), Hugh Futcher (Cab Driver), Patricia Hayes (Mrs Beasley), Harry Locke (Porter), Elizabeth Knight (Nurse Willing), Alexandra Dane (Stout Woman), William Mervyn (Lord Paragon), Lucy Griffiths (Headphones Lady), Gwendolyn Watts (Night Sister), Jenny Counsell (Night Nurse), Valerie Leon (Deirdre), Frank Singuineau (Second Porter), Valerie Van Ost (Outpatients Sister), Simon Cain (X-Ray Operator), Elspeth March (Hospital Board Member), Valerie Shute (Nurse), Ann Lancaster (Miss Armitage), Georgina Simpson (Men's Ward Nurse), Eric Rogers (Bandleader), Donald Bissett (Patient), Bob Todd (Pump Patient), Heather Emmanuel (Plump Native Girl), Shakira Baksh (Thinned-Down Native Girl), Yutte Stensgaard (Trolley Nurse), George Roderick (Waiter), Rupert Evans (Stunt Orderly), Billy Cornelius (Patient in Plaster)

Crew: Director Gerald Thomas, Screenplay Talbot Rothwell, Producer Peter Rogers, Music Eric Rogers, Director of Photography Ernest Steward, Editor Alfred Roome, Assistant Editor Jack Gardner, Art Director John Blezard, Assistant Director Ivor Powell, Production Manager Jack Swinburne, Camera Operator James Bawden, Continuity Susanna Merry, Make-Up Geoffrey Rodway, Hairdresser Stella Rivers, Costume Designer Anna Duse, Sound Recordists Bill Daniels & Ken Barker, Dubbing Editor Colin Miller (Rank Organisation, 1969, Eastmancolor, 89m, A/PG)

Alternatively: 'Where There's a Pill There's a Way' or 'The Bowels are Ringing' or 'If You Say It's Your

Thermometer I'll Have to Believe You, But It's a Funny Place to Put It'

DVD: 2003 (Carlton, 3711503383, SE)

Story: When Dr Nookey (Jim Dale) is sent to the distant Beatific Islands, he makes a startling medical discovery that he hopes will bring fame and fortune...

Notable Lines: Barbara Windsor: 'I have to watch my figure.' Jim Dale: 'Well, if I may say so, it's well worth watching.' Barbara Windsor: 'Oh! If I don't, I blow up like a balloon.' Jim Dale: 'That's all right. I know a good game with balloons.' / Kenneth Williams: 'In medical parlance, you're up the alimentary canal without a paddle.' / Sid James: 'May the fertility of Sumarkus swell your coconuts.' / Jim Dale: 'Hmm, it's a good skeleton. Did the last doctor leave it here?' Sid James: 'That *is* the last doctor.' / Kenneth Williams: 'By the time I've finished with him he'll never practise medicine again. He'll be lucky to get a job curing kippers!' / Hattie Jacques: 'All he seems to think about is whisky and sex.' Jim Dale: 'From where he comes from, they can't get soda.'

Key Scene: For sheer *Benny Hill* obviousness, I nominate Valerie Leon offering her services (gulp) to newly appointed doctor Jim Dale. Oo-er missus.

Observations: When Kenneth Williams and Joan Sims are walking along outside the new clinic, a close-up shows them standing still.

All Dragged Up: Charles Hawtrey goes undercover as Lady Puddleton.

Location: Maidenhead Town Hall, Berks.

Review: A swift return to the *Doctor* scenario indicates that the *Carry On* team was getting short of ideas. But *Again Doctor* is stylistically so different to the Frankie Howerd vehicle that a comparison is hardly justified. With its exotic island location, it has more in common with the next film, *Up the Jungle*.

None of the main three regulars seem comfortable in their roles. Charles Hawtrey is oddly miscast as a serious figure of authority, although, being Hawtrey, he does play to the camera whenever he can; Kenneth Williams is given a part that is too suave and worldly-wise to be particularly funny (in his *Diaries* he considered his performance 'remarkably authoritative') and Sid James is separated from the action for so long that when he does interact with the regulars, it's too little too late. Jim Dale tries valiantly to hold the whole thing together but with little success. Barbara Windsor famously wears almost next to nothing (proving that some people really do look better with their clothes on), while Joan Sims gets to display an impressive cleavage. It's a shame that Sims was often pigeon-holed as the fusty housewife, because, as she demonstrates here, she could ooze sex when she chose to.

There are some good jokes (the native drums sending the latest football results), but the film looks tired and cheap. The decision to jump between three disparate locations slows the pace down, while the farcical clinic scenes at the end just peter out into nothing.

Verdict: The formula is looking extremely threadbare now, so my diagnosis is a mere **2/5**.

19) Carry On Up the Jungle (1970)

Cast: Frankie Howerd (Professor Inigo Tinkle), Sid James (Bill Boosey), Joan Sims (Lady Evelyn Bagley), Kenneth Connor (Claude Chumley), Charles Hawtrey (King Tonka/Walter Bagley), Bernard Bresslaw (Upsidasi), Terry Scott (Cecil/Ug), Jacki Piper (June), Valerie Leon (Leda), Edwina Carroll (Nerda), Reuben Martin (Gorilla), Danny Daniels (Nosha Chief), Yemi Ajibade (Witch Doctor), Lincoln Webb (Nosha with Girl), Heather Emmanuel (Pregnant Lubi), Verna Lucille MacKenzie (Gong Lubi), Valerie Moore, Cathi March (Lubi Lieutenants), Nina Baden-Semper (Girl Nosha), Roy Stewart, John Hamilton, Chris Konyils, Willie Jonah (Noshas)

Crew: Director Gerald Thomas, Screenplay Talbot Rothwell, Producer Peter Rogers, Music Eric Rogers, Director of Photography Ernest Steward, Editor Alfred Roome, Art Director Alex Vetchinsky, Assistant Editor Jack Gardner, Assistant Director Jack Causey, Production Manager Jack Swinburne, Camera Operator James Bawden, Continuity Josephine Knowles, Make-Up Geoffrey Rodway, Hairdresser Stella Rivers, Costume Designer Courtenay Elliott, Sound Recordists Robert T MacPhee & Ken Barker, Dubbing Editor Colin Miller (Rank, March 1970, Eastmancolor, 89m, A/PG)

Alternatively: 'The African Queens' or 'Stop Beating About the Bush' or 'Show Me Your Waterhole and I'll Show You Mine'

DVD: 2003 (Carlton, 3711503433, SE)

Story: On the trail of the Oozalum Bird in deepest,

darkest Africa, Professor Tinkle (Frankie Howerd) and Claude Chumley (Kenneth Connor) stumble across an Amazonian race who are in desperate need of men...

Notable Lines: Frankie Howerd: 'You don't find Golden Crested Tits here in Africa. An occasional black one, maybe...' / Sid James: 'Blimey, look at them rings! Ain't they whoppers?' Joan Sims: 'I have a matching pair as well.' Sid James: 'And don't think I hadn't noticed that!' / Bernard Bresslaw: 'He's dead, boss.' Frankie Howerd: 'Oh dear, I do hope it's nothing serious.' / Kenneth Connor: 'This is Africa — a land of unbridled passion. Let's get our bridles off!' / Frankie Howerd: 'I'm flabbergasted. My gast has never been so flabbered.' / Sid James: 'We're going in that pot.' Kenneth Connor: 'Us? Stewed?' Sid James: 'Not a chance. Stone-cold sober.'

Key Scene: Charles Hawtrey doing cod baby talk in the sublime flashback-within-a-flashback scene ('What a cow-sy-wowsy.').

Observations: The slingshot used by Terry Scott appears from nowhere.

Location: Windsor, Berks.

Review: In a botched attempt to repeat the success of *Khyber*, the crew returns to the British Colonialism theme with intrepid explorers and backward savages in this cheap-looking spoof of all things H Rider Haggard. After an excellent opening theme (all scary drumbeats and the classic refrain, 'Oompa, oompa, stick it up your jumper!'), we find Frankie Howerd giving a lecture in a draughty church hall. So good, so *Carry On Doctor*. Then we move into a flashback – one of the very few *Carry On*s that uses this device, incidentally – and cue a blacked-up Bernard Bresslaw, grainy old stock footage and an hour and a half of sex jokes (bestiality, incest, impotency – it's all there). The infamous dinner scene says it all really, as Joan Sims receives the attentions of an inquisitive snake up her bloomers and assumes it's her male colleagues. This broad obsession with sex would continue with the remainder of the series, culminating in *Emmannuelle*, in which a variation of the aforementioned snake scene appears. That's not to say the *Carry On*s had avoided the subject before, but with *Up the Jungle* the jokes became more laboured and explicit (as in Sid James' self-raising gun).

As to the cast, Frankie Howerd steals the picture, as he did with *Doctor*, while Charles Hawtrey provides excellent comic relief as the frightfully refined King Tonka, leader of the gorgeous Lubi-Dubbies. 'Oh no, it's the wife!' he exclaims on seeing Joan Sims. Terry Scott is very good too, wholeheartedly slipping into a comedy Tarzan role that seems tailor-made for him.

Dire moments abound though. The speeded-up sequence with a man in a gorilla suit is embarrassing, as is the scene where Kenneth Connor spies on Joan Sims' body double in the shower. The studio-bound jungle is cheap, the Oozalum Bird is obviously a puppet, and the 'in and out of tents' farce is as risible as the similar sequence in the film version of *Are You Being Served?* (1977) – and we all know how terrible that was. None of this would matter if the film was funny, but it is simply just too childish and obvious to raise much of a laugh.

Verdict: For being a poor man's *Khyber*, I give this just **2/5**.

20) Carry On Loving (1970)

Cast: Sid James (Sidney Bliss), Hattie Jacques (Sophie 'Bliss'), Kenneth Williams (Percival Snooper), Charles Hawtrey (James Bedsop), Joan Sims (Esme Crowfoot), Terry Scott (Terence Philpot), Jacki Piper (Sally Martin), Richard O'Callaghan (Bertie Muffet), Bernard Bresslaw (Gripper Burke), Imogen Hassall (Jenny Grubb), Patsy Rowlands (Miss Dempsey), Peter Butterworth ('Dr Crippen'), Julian Holloway (Adrian), Bill Pertwee (Bartender), Kenny Lynch (Bus Conductor), Janet Mahoney (Gay), Joan Hickson (Mrs Grubb), Ann Way (Aunt Victoria Grubb), Gordon Richardson (Uncle Ernest Grubb), Hilda Barry (Grandma Grubb), Bart Allison (Grandpa Grubb), Dorothea Phillips (Aunt Beatrice Grubb), Colin Vancao (Wilberforce Grubb), Bill Maynard (Mr Dreery), Patricia Franklin (Mrs Dreery), Amelia Bayntun (Corset Lady), Tom Clegg (Trainer), Lucy Griffiths (Woman), Valerie Shute (Girlfriend), Mike Grady (Boyfriend), Anthony Sagar (Patient), Harry Shacklock (Lavatory Attendant), Derek Francis (Bishop), Alexandra Dane (Emily), Philip Stone (Robinson), Sonny Farrar (Violinist), Josie Bradly (Pianist), Anna Karen (Wife), Lauri Lupino Lane (Husband), Gavin Reed (Window Dresser), Joe Cornelius (Second), Len Lowe (Maitre d'Hotel), Fred Griffiths (Taxi Driver), Ronnie Brody (Henry), Robert Russell (Policeman)

Crew: Director Gerald Thomas, Screenplay Talbot Rothwell, Producer Peter Rogers, Music Eric Rogers, Director of Photography Ernest Steward, Editor Alfred Roome, Art Director Lionel Couch, Assistant Editor Jack Gardner, Assistant Director David Bracknell, Assistant Art Director William Alexander, Production Manager Jack

Swinburne, Camera Operator James Bawden, Continuity Josephine Knowles, Make-Up Geoffrey Rodway, Hairdresser Stella Rivers, Costume Designer Courtenay Elliott, Sound Recordists JWN Daniel & Ken Barker, Dubbing Editor Marcel Durham, Set Dresser Peter Howitt (Rank, September 1970, Eastmancolor, 88m, A/PG)

Alternatively: 'It's Not What You Feel, It's the Way That You Feel It' or 'Two's Company but Three's Quite Good Fun Too' or 'Love Is a Four-Letter Word' or 'It's Just One Thing on Top of Another'

DVD: 2003 (Carlton, 3711503463, SE)

Story: In Much Snogging-on-the-Green, happily 'married' couple Sidney and Sophie Bliss (Sid James and Hattie Jacques) run a profitable computer-dating agency with a difference – they don't have a computer...

Notable Lines: Hattie Jacques: 'The young woman at the tobacconist – you must have vetted her at least 50 times.' Sid James: 'Oh Gawd, I only keep going in there for my shag.' / Sid James: 'If (miniskirts) get any shorter, they'll have two more cheeks to powder.' / Imogen Hassall: 'I've got a modelling job in half an hour. It's a new kind of body stocking and I can't get out of it.' Sid James: 'Come here and I'll get you out of it.' / Imogen Hassall (to cat): 'Shoo, Cooking Fat, shoo!'... Terry Scott: 'They can't call him that, surely?' Imogen Hassall: 'Well, that's what it sounds like.' / Joan Sims: 'I know you've found someone else, I know it. I can feel it.' Kenneth Williams: 'Well, stop feeling it.'

Key Scene: Sid James makes a great performance of putting Richard O'Callaghan's card into this huge *Blake's Seven*-style computer to find a suitable match, when in reality all he does is push it through a hole in the wall into the next room where Hattie Jacques picks a random match out of a shoebox.

Observations: Sonny Farrar seems to have trouble breaking his violin across the top of Josie Bradly's head in the custard pie scene.

Location: Windsor, Berks.

Review: The tone of this film – which should have been called *Carry On Lusting* – is immediately set by the double-decker bus advertising the stage play *Sex* ('Twice Nightly!') and the groping of a lusty young couple on the top deck. These two appear several times in a vague attempt to bring structure to the rambling narrative, but it's such a messy film that the idea is pointless.

The cast try their best with a weak script, but you can't blame them if the results aren't up to much. Kenneth Williams has no real character to speak of, and Joan Sims is wasted in the relatively small part of Sid's 'bit on the side', the dowdy 'corset fitter' who lives in the shadow of her wrestler husband Bernard Bresslaw. Charles Hawtrey shines as the unlikely private detective (note the eyeholes he cuts in his newspaper), who gets accused of cottaging, while Sid James and Hattie Jacques replay their loveless marriage from *Cabby*. Patsy Rowlands gets her best role in the series as the landlady who lusts after Kenneth Williams – her transformation into sultry temptress is hilarious – while new boy Richard O'Callaghan is cast in the vacant Jim Dale role as clumsy virginal nerd. Julian Holloway is saddled with an even grubbier character than usual, and the sequence in Jacki Piper's flat with Terry Scott (foreshadowing his lustful persona in *Matron*) attempting to seduce the outstanding Imogen Hassall is the closest the series got to *Confessions Of...* coupling.

The crux of the film is the tension between old and young generations in the 'swinging 60s'. Hence we have the dark, Victorian atmosphere of the Grubbs' family home (aided by a rendition of the third movement of Chopin's Piano Sonata No.2 in B flat minor, the famous March Funèbre) neatly contrasting with Vicki Piper's trendy Art Deco flat, with its black and white furnishings and prints by (ironically) Victorian illustrator Aubrey Beardsley. This emphasis on conservative morality versus the new 'permissive' society arguably makes this entry the most dated *Carry On* film of all, more so even than the archaic antics of *Sergeant* or *Nurse*. In trying to side with a fashionable younger audience (rather than belittle it as the makers did in *Camping*), the *Carry On* producers just show their age even more. Odd then, that they end the film with the oldest slapstick routine possible – a custard pie fight.

Verdict: Crude and unfunny, I give this limp offering 2/5.

21) Carry On Henry (1971)

Cast: Sid James (King Henry VIII), Charles Hawtrey (Sir Roger de Lodgerley), Kenneth Williams (Thomas Cromwell), Terry Scott (Cardinal Wolsey), Joan Sims (Queen Marie of Normandy), Barbara Windsor (Bettina), Kenneth Connor (Lord Hampton of Wick), Julian Holloway (Sir Thomas), Patsy Rowlands (Anne of

Cléves), Peter Gilmore (King Francis of France), Peter Butterworth (Charles, Earl of Bristol), Julian Orchard (Duc de Poncenay), Gertan Klauber (Bidet), Margaret Nolan (Buxom Girl), Derek Francis (Farmer), William Mervyn (Physician), Alan Curtis (Conte di Pisa), John Bluthal (Moisha Montmorency), David Davenport (Major Domo), Bill Maynard (Guy Fawkes), Norman Chappell (First Plotter), Douglas Ridley (Second Plotter), Leon Greene, Dave Prowse (Torturers), Monika Dietrich (Catherine Howard), Billy Cornelius (Guard), Marjie Lawrence (Serving Maid), William McGuirk (Flunky), Jane Cardew (Second Wife), Valerie Shute (Maid), Peter Rigby, Trevor Roberts, Peter Munt (Courtiers)

Crew: Director Gerald Thomas, Screenplay Talbot Rothwell, Producer Peter Rogers, Music Eric Rogers, Director of Photography Alan Hume, Editor Alfred Roome, Art Director Lionel Couch, Assistant Editor Jack Gardner, Assistant Director David Bracknell, Assistant Art Director William Alexander, Production Manager Jack Swinburne, Camera Assistant Derek Browne, Continuity Rita Davison, Make-Up Geoffrey Rodway, Hairdresser Stella Rivers, Costume Designer Courtenay Elliott, Sound Recordists Danny Daniels & Ken Barker, Dubbing Editor Brian Holland, Set Dresser Peter Howitt (Rank, February 1971, Eastmancolor, 89m, A/PG)

Alternatively: 'Mind My Chopper'

DVD: 2003 (Carlton, 3711503413, SE)

Story: Henry VIII's (Sid James') attempts at seducing two previously unrecorded wives go sadly awry...

Notable Lines: Kenneth Williams: 'She always was a weakly woman, Sire.' Sid James: 'You're telling me – once weekly!' / Sid James: 'That settles it – get her annulled.' Terry Scott: 'An old what, Sire?' / Kenneth Williams: 'We've not had the pleasure of your company for a meal as yet.' Joan Sims: 'No, I've been having it in my room with Sir Roger.' / Joan Sims: 'What did you do with all your other wives in bed?' Sid James: 'Ah, let me think. Now then, with old Jane we used to play noughts and crosses.' Joan Sims: 'Noughts and crosses?' Sid James: 'Yes, I kept giving her nought and she got cross.' / Sid James: 'We're proud of our royal legs, Moisha – we like the ladies of the court to marvel at their length.' John Bluthal: 'Your Majesty, if I make the skirt any higher, they won't be marvelling at the length of your legs.' Sid James: 'Oh, that reminds me, I need a bit more length on the hose.' John Bluthal: 'Your Majesty is much too modest.' / Sid James: 'I shouldn't have to tell you that, speaking royally, my mint has a hole in it.' Kenneth Williams: 'We could raise a bit more by taxation.' Sid James: 'Taxation? Everything's taxed to the hilt as it is – even swords.' / Kenneth Williams: 'I am known as Cromwell the Considerate.' Joan Sims: 'You? What about all those poor martyrs you had burned at the stake last week?' Kenneth Williams: 'What about that?' Joan Sims: 'You call that considerate?' Kenneth Williams: 'Why of course, didn't I go round every one of them personally and say, "How do you like your stake?"' / Sid James: 'May I have the pleasure?' Barbara Windsor: 'Oh no, I only came here to dance.' / Sid James: 'There must be an easier way to earn a loving!' / Sid James: 'Arise, Hampton, Prince of Berks.'

Key Scene: Just when Sid James is about to get his end away with Joan Sims, she pops some garlic in her mouth and he jumps back like a scalded cat.

Observations: At the end of Charles Hawtrey's first scene, he leaves Henry's bedchamber speaking some lines, but without opening his lips. Terry Scott is in two places at once – at the execution and in the chapel. A shot of the baby is missing at the end (presumably it would have shown the features of Charles Hawtrey), while Joan Sims' labour is the shortest in film history. Costumes were reused from the 1969 Richard Burton film *Anne of the Thousand Days* (hence the original alternative title, *Anne of a Thousand Lays*). The guillotine was named after Joseph Ignace Guillotin in 1789, and so when Sid James mentions it here, he's about 250 years too early. Guy Fawkes' Gunpowder Plot is too early as well – by 65 years (1605, as opposed to *Henry's* setting of 1540) – but not as bad as the cavemen in *Cleo*!

Locations: Windsor Great Park and Long Walk, Windsor, Berks.

Review: Back on form after their last effort, the *Carry On* team proves once again its mastery of the historical setting, thanks to a wonderfully bawdy script by Talbot Rothwell and enthusiastic playing by all the cast, especially Sid James in a role he seems born to play. Kenneth Williams and Terry Scott (who has the painful task of smuggling parchments to France where the sun don't shine) make a satisfying double act, while Joan Sims is delightful as the randy, garlic-eating French Queen Marie. Charles Hawtrey, playing the superbly named Roger de Lodgerley, is on the receiving end of various *Loony Toons*-style tortures, and Barbara Windsor once more gets 'em out for the lads. It's a pity that Patsy Rowlands is only given a few moments of screen time, but we can't have everything.

The historical backdrop is splendidly brought to life by realistic sets and borrowed costumes, and although the script groans with puns and put-downs, it's also thick with plot twists and intrigue, which is quite an achievement. Nods are given to previous successes *Cleo* ('Frannie!' 'Gracey!') and *Khyber* (the 'up yours!' joke sees the light of day again), and there are some great pseudo-historical gags, such as Kenneth Connor's splendidly delivered motto 'non fartum contra tonightum' – 'fight not against thunder'. All the old BBC Classic Serial clichés are here, such as the torture chamber (with a 'vacant' sign on the Iron Maiden), the riotous banqueting scene and the heaving bosoms and mammoth codpieces – it's *Blackadder II* 15 years early!

The emphasis on sex is still prevalent, but at least here, with its tale of an oversexed monarch, it has some relevance. And – despite seeing Barbara Windsor in the nude and Margaret Nolan falling out of her costume – it's all done, as Kenny Everett would say, 'in the best possible taste'. Interestingly, Kenneth Williams in his *Diaries* vacillated on his view of the film. He originally called the script 'abysmal', yet when it was shown on TV in 1979, he wrote, 'amazing how well this was made! Everyone in it was competent and the sheer *look* of the thing was very professional.' Years later in 1988, after another TV airing, he complained about its 'truly chronic dialogue', and went on to castigate it as 'a collection of such rubbish you're amazed it could ever have been stuck together. Only an audience of illiterates could ever have found this tripe amusing.'

Verdict: I watched this the same time as Kenneth Williams in 1979, at the tender age of 12, and delivered the following comment in *my* diary: 'Watched *Carry On*

Henry. It wasn't as funny as the others.' Well, like Kenneth Williams, I've since changed my mind – it *is* as funny as the others, and more so. **5/5**.

22) Carry On at Your Convenience (1971)

Cast: Sid James (Sid Plummer), Kenneth Williams (WC Boggs), Charles Hawtrey (Charles Coote), Joan Sims (Chloe Moore), Hattie Jacques (Beattie Plummer), Bill Maynard (Fred Moore), Bernard Bresslaw (Bernie Hulke), Kenneth Cope (Vic Spanner), Renée Houston (Agatha Spanner), Richard O'Callaghan (Lewis Boggs), Jacki Piper (Myrtle Plummer), Patsy Rowlands (Hortence Withering), Davy Kaye (Benny), Marianne Stone (Maud), Margaret Nolan (Popsy), Geoffrey Hughes (Willie), Hugh Futcher (Ernie), Simon Cain (Barman), Amelia Bayntun (Mrs Spragg), Leon Greene (Chef), Harry Towb (Film Doctor), Shirley Stelfox (Bunny Waitress), Peter Burton (Hotel Manager), Julian Holloway (Roger), Jan Rossini (Hoopla Girl), Philip Stone (Mr Bulstrode)

Crew: Director Gerald Thomas, Screenplay Talbot Rothwell, Producer Peter Rogers, Music Eric Rogers, Director of Photography Ernest Steward, Editor Alfred Roome, Art Director Lionel Couch, Assistant Editor Jack Gardner, Assistant Director David Bracknell, Assistant Art Director William Alexander, Production Manager Jack Swinburne, Camera Operator James Bawden, Continuity Rita Davidson, Make-Up Geoffrey Rodway, Hairdresser Stella Rivers, Costume Designer Courtenay Elliott, Sound Recordists Danny Daniel & Ken Barker, Dubbing Editor Brian Holland, Toilets by Royal Doulton Sanitary Potteries (Rank Organisation, December 1971, Eastmancolor, 90m, A/PG)

Alternatively: 'Down the Spout' or 'Ladies Please Be Seated' or 'Up the Workers' or 'Labour Relations Are the People Who Come to See You When You're Having a Baby'

DVD: 2003 (Carlton, 3711503453, SE)

Story: At WC Boggs & Co, the unions are revolting...

Notable Lines: Sid James: 'Very slender this pedestal, isn't it?' Charles Hawtrey: 'It's streamlined!' Sid James: 'What for? Wind resistance?' / Sid James: 'I don't see the use of them. It's easy enough to wash your feet in the bath.' Richard O'Callaghan: 'Bidets aren't for washing your feet in, Mr Plummer.' Sid James: 'What else then? Are they for dogs to drink out of?' (Richard O'Callaghan whispers in Sid's ear) Sid James: 'Get away! If it's for that, then you can always stand on your head under the shower!' / Sid James (to bird): 'She spoils you to budgery, do you know that?' / Bernard Bresslaw: 'You're a miserable little leader.' / Kenneth Cope: 'You didn't have to come out with me today, you know.' Bernard Bresslaw: 'No, and I can't wait not to come out with you tomorrow either.' / Kenneth Williams: 'She's not getting any younger.' Sid James: 'She's not getting any!' / Patsy Rowlands (to Kenneth Williams): 'Oh don't worry, I know what a man looks like, you know – and you're not all that much different.'

Key Scene: Patsy Rowlands' fumbling attempt to seduce the terrified Kenneth Williams; while the latter's delivery of, 'Hortence!' is quite spectacular.

Observations: Harry Towb's American accent is a mixture of Irish and deepest Somerset. 'The Chippit Inn' appears to be the same location as the clinic in *Again Doctor* and Chayste Place in *Camping*. On the return journey from Brighton, the works coach stops off at seven (real) pubs – the Red Lion, King's Head (Albourne), Cricketers Inn, Royal Naval Arms, The Seagull, The Trout Inn and The Man in Space.

All Dragged Up: Sid James as a fortune-teller.

Location: Brighton and environs, East Sussex.

Review: While *Loving* is a generational comedy, *Convenience* is a class comedy; but it makes the mistake of mocking the very audience at which the films are primarily aimed – the working class. So we have Kenneth Cope as the tin-pot trade union leader, all bluster and offended dignity (like Norman Chappell's character from *Cabby*) pitted against Sid James' fatherly warm-hearted factory boss. It's clear which side the filmmakers are taking, and the low box-office takings indicate the anti-trade union stance was not a popular one with the general public.

That said, there are plenty of good things about *Convenience*. Charles Hawtrey is all flowery cravats and jaunty hats (during the Brighton scenes he looks uncannily like Quentin Crisp), Patsy Rowlands is wonderful as the repressed secretary to the nervous Kenneth Williams, and Joan Sims gives a sympathetic performance as the liberated factory worker with a soft spot for Sid James. The latter hitches up yet again with Hattie Jacques for an uninteresting subplot about a talking budgie, but there's a touching scene with Sid and Joan as estranged lovers, their frustrations achingly conveyed, that adds poignancy to their relationship. Renée Houston is foul-mouthed ('crap,' 'sod' and 'bastard' lower the tone) and the less said about

Bernard Bresslaw and Kenneth Cope the better. What saves the film is the trip to Brighton. Here the cast let their hair down and re-enact true Donald McGill postcard scenarios, a foretaste of the joys of *Girls* two years later. Kenneth Williams is especially amusing as he prances around Brighton Pier spouting dirty limericks, and it's delightful to watch the cast where they properly belong – at the end of a pier.

Verdict: Despite the lovely seaside sojourn, the film only gets a bog standard **3/5**.

23) Carry On Matron (1972)

Cast: Kenneth Williams (Sir Bernard Cutting), Sid James (Sid Carter), Hattie Jacques (Matron), Charles Hawtrey (Dr Francis A Goode), Joan Sims (Mrs Tidey), Kenneth Connor (Mr Tidey), Bernard Bresslaw (Ernie Bragg), Barbara Windsor (Nurse Susan Ball), Terry Scott (Dr Prodd), Kenneth Cope (Cyril Carter), Jacki Piper (Sister), Bill Maynard (Freddy), Patsy Rowlands (Evelyn Banks), Valerie Leon (Jane Darling), Robin Hunter (Mr Darling), Zena Clifton (Au Pair), Derek Francis (Arthur), Wendy Richard (Miss Willing), Amelia Bayntun (Mrs Jenkins), Brian Osborne (Ambulance Driver), Gwendolyn Watts (Frances Kemp), Valerie Shute (Miss Smethurst), Margaret Nolan (Mrs Tucker), Michael Nightingale (Pearson), Bill Kenwright (Reporter), Jack Douglas (Twitching Father), Madeline Smith (Mrs Pullitt), Juliet Harmer (Mrs Bentley), Gilly Grant (Nurse in Bath), Lindsay March, Laura Collins (Nurses)

Crew: Director Gerald Thomas, Screenplay Talbot Rothwell, Producer Peter Rogers, Music Eric Rogers,

Director of Photography Ernest Steward, Editor Alfred Roome, Art Director Lionel Couch, Assistant Editor Jack Gardner, Assistant Director Bert Batt, Assistant Art Director William Alexander, Production Manager Jack Swinburne, Camera Operator James Bawden, Continuity Joy Mercer, Make-Up Geoffrey Rodway, Hairdresser Stella Rivers, Costume Designer Courtenay Elliott, Sound Recordists Danny Daniel & Ken Barker, Dubbing Editor Peter Best, Set Dresser Peter Lamont, Wardrobe Mistresses Vi Murray & Maggie Lewin (Rank, May 1972, Eastmancolor, 87m, A/PG)

Alternatively: 'From Here to Maternity' or 'Familiarity Breeds' or 'Womb at the Top' or 'The Preggars Opera'

DVD: 2003 (Carlton, 3711503353, SE)

Story: Sid Carter (Sid James) plans a daring theft of contraceptive pills from the Finisham Maternity Hospital. But he doesn't count on his accomplice son (Kenneth Cope) falling for a pretty young nurse (Barbara Windsor)…

Notable Lines: Hattie Jacques: 'I nearly forgot – your mail.' Kenneth Williams: 'Yes I am – and I can prove it, d'ya hear? Prove it!' / Charles Hawtrey: 'I call (my wife) Hamlet because she thinks she's a Great Dane.' / Hattie Jacques: 'I'm a simple woman with simple tastes and I want to be wooed.' Kenneth Williams: 'Ooh, you can be as wooed as you like with me!' / Charles Hawtrey: 'I beg your pardon – we've never had so much as an ounce of a bounce!'

Key Scene: The out-of-the-blue argument about the 73

bus route is sheer bliss; a wonderfully surreal Eddie Izzard-style diversion from the main plot, very amusingly performed. 'Down the Balls Pond Road and into Islington,' says Bresslaw seriously. Sublime.

Observations: Hattie Jacques corpses when she is swatting Kenneth Williams with her flowers. The explosion goes off before Sid James twists the detonator.

All Dragged Up: Kenneth Cope as a female nurse and Bernard Bresslaw as a pregnant patient.

Location: Heatherwood Hospital and environs, Ascot, Berks; Denham, Bucks.

Review: This is unashamedly my favourite medical *Carry On*. It has a strong plotline, it's got Kenneth Cope as a sympathetic cross-dressing criminal, and it features the best-ever pairing of Kenneth Williams and Charles Hawtrey. Plus the fact that Sid James plays a crook and disguises himself as 'Dr Zhivago' complete with dodgy multilingual phrases ('Gracias, enchante'), Hattie Jacques does her best Matron (with blonde hair for a change), Jack 'like him or loathe him' Douglas is introduced into the fold, Gilly Grant shows us her soapy assets, and it ends with a very impressive ambulance crash. A heady brew indeed.

Star of the film is Kenneth Williams, in his finest contemporary role. He is simply brilliant as the neurotic hypochondriac who thinks he's turning into a woman. His mannerisms and body language throughout are hilarious, and when he and Hawtrey (playing a psychiatrist, for goodness sake!) share a scene together they forge comedy gold. Their best scene starts with them both at loggerheads until Williams suddenly realises that they're fellow Newts (read Freemasons), and they get all pally: 'I am a Great Salamander Newt of the Watford Pond!' exclaims Williams pompously. Hawtrey shares a hilarious moment with Hattie Jacques too, as they coyly meet in her room to watch *The Surgeon* on TV. His plaintive comments about his mad wife ('she'd rather curl up on the hearth rug with a good bone') are beautifully delivered, and he manages to bring a rare element of pathos into the role, as well as being screamingly funny.

Verdict: For being the best medical *Carry On*, I give it a rollicking **5/5**.

'I'm in the Pit!' (1972–1992)

24) Carry On Abroad (1972)

Cast: Sid James (Vic Flange), Kenneth Williams (Stuart Farquhar), Charles Hawtrey (Eustace Tuttle), Joan Sims (Cora Flange), Kenneth Connor (Stanley Blunt), June Whitfield (Evelyn Blunt), Hattie Jacques (Floella), Peter Butterworth (Pepe), Barbara Windsor (Sadie Tomkins), Bernard Bresslaw (Brother Bernard), Jimmy Logan (Bert Conway), Sally Geeson (Lily), Gail Grainger (Moira), Carol Hawkins (Marge), Ray Brooks (Georgio), John Clive (Robin), David Kernan (Nicholas), Patsy Rowlands (Miss Dobbs), Derek Francis (Brother Martin), Jack Douglas (Harry), Amelia Bayntun (Mrs Tuttle), Alan Curtis (Police Chief), Hugh Futcher (Jailer), Gertan Klauber (Postcard Seller), Brian Osborne (Stallholder), Olga Lowe (Madame Fifi)

Crew: Director Gerald Thomas, Screenplay Talbot Rothwell, Producer Peter Rogers, Music Eric Rogers, Director of Photography Alan Hume, Editor Alfred Roome, Art Director Lionel Couch, Assistant Editor Jack Gardner, Assistant Director David Bracknell, Assistant Art Director Bill Bennison, Production Manager Jack Swinburne, Camera Operator Jimmy Devis, Continuity Joy Mercer, Make-Up Geoffrey Rodway, Hairdresser Stella Rivers, Costume Designer Courtenay Elliott, Sound

Recordists Taffy Haines & Ken Barker, Sound Editor Peter Best, Set Dresser Don Picton, Technical Adviser Sun Tan Lo Tion (Rank, December 1972, Eastmancolor, 88m, A/PG)

Alternatively: 'What a Package' or 'It's All In' or 'Swiss Hols in the Snow'

DVD: 2003 (Carlton, 3711503363, SE)

Story: Stuart Farquhar (Kenneth Williams) leads a group of holidaymakers on a disastrous package tour to the holiday resort of Els Bells…

Notable Lines: Kenneth Williams: 'I'm the representative of WundaTours – Stuart Farquhar.' Peter Butterworth: 'Stupid what?' / Kenneth Williams: 'Ah excellent, the wine. Spanish-type Australian French Burgundy, product of Hong Kong.' / Kenneth Williams: 'Do you believe in free love?' Joan Sims: 'Well, I'm certainly not paying for it!' / Barbara Windsor: 'You only want one thing from me.' Jimmy Logan: 'That's not true – I'm quite happy to have the lot!' / Peter Butterworth: 'Please excusings! Slight technical hitchings!'

Key Scene: The top-and-tailing scenes in the pub are nicely played, especially the delightful ending as everyone piles back in to relive their holiday experiences. It's good that Hawtrey's final appearance should end on this celebratory high note.

Location: Slough, Berks.

Review: Kenneth Williams says in his *Diaries* of 18 April 1972: 'Though it was the first day (on *Abroad*), there was an air of staleness over everything. A feeling of 'I have been here before' and I thought the acting standard was rather bad throughout.' Words I can add little to – *Abroad* is a plotless one-joke film in which a group of aging comedy actors resurrect old characters and search for a decent line. Most of the jokes revolve around the half-finished hotel and, as you would expect, there is very little action in a film that concentrates on people sitting in a hotel lobby or sunbathing on a veranda. You never get the feeling that the cast are in another country so – like *Cruising* – the intended exotic atmosphere just seems cheap and tacky. Charles Hawtrey mirrors his real-life self by playing an alcoholic (this was his final *Carry On* contribution, due to his erratic behaviour on set), Jimmy Logan gives a performance that brings new meaning to the word 'unsubtle' and Kenneth Williams is all silly voice and face-pulling. Poor Hattie Jacques is given the unpromising role of a haranguing cook, sister to the (excellent as ever) Peter Butterworth, and there is a rather desultory attempt to imitate the ending of *Khyber* with Butterworth running around madly while the hotel collapses – but this is done with such a lack of conviction that it makes even the tawdriest 1970s disaster movie look good by comparison. (Having said that, an earlier glass-shot of the uncompleted hotel is quietly impressive).

Verdict: A routine effort with few redeeming features, I give it **2/5**.

25) Carry On Girls (1973)

Cast: Sid James (Sidney Fiddler), Barbara Windsor (Hope Springs/Muriel Bloggs), Kenneth Connor (Mayor Frederick Bumble), Joan Sims (Connie Philpotts), Bernard

Bresslaw (Peter Potter), Peter Butterworth (Admiral), June Whitfield (Augusta Prodworthy), Patsy Rowlands (Mildred Bumble), Jack Douglas (William), Robin Askwith (Larry), Joan Hickson (Mrs Dukes), Valerie Leon (Paula Perkins), Margaret Nolan (Dawn Brakes), Angela Grant (Miss Bangor), Sally Geeson (Debra), Wendy Richard (Ida Downe), David Lodge (Police Inspector), Billy Cornelius (Constable), Jimmy Logan (Cecil Gaybody), Arnold Ridley (Alderman Pratt), Patricia Franklin (Rosemary), Bill Pertwee (Fire Chief), Marianne Stone (Miss Drew), Brenda Cowling (Matron), Mavis Fyson (Francis Cake), Laraine Humphreys (Eileen Denby), Caroline Whitaker (Mary Parker), Pauline Peart (Gloria Winch), Barbara Wise (Julia Oates), Carol Wyler (Maureen Darcy), Edward Palmer (Elderly Resident), Michael Nightingale (City Gent), Elsie Winsor (Cloakroom Attendant), Brian Osborne (First Citizen), Hugh Futcher (Second Citizen), Nick Hobbs (Stunt Double)

Crew: Director Gerald Thomas, Screenplay Talbot Rothwell, Producer Peter Rogers, Music Eric Rogers, Director of Photography Alan Hume, Editor Alfred Roome, Art Director Robert Jones, Assistant Editors Jack Gardner & Ken Behrens, Assistant Director Jack Causey, Production Manager Roy Goddard, Camera Operator Jimmy Devis, Continuity Marjorie Lavelly, Make-Up Geoffrey Rodway, Hairdresser Stella Rivers, Costume Designer Courtenay Elliott, Sound Recordists Paul Lemare & Ken Barker, Dubbing Editor Patrick Foster, Set Dresser Kenneth McCallum Tait, Title Sketches by 'Larry' (Rank, November 1973, Eastmancolor, 88m, A/PG)

DVD: 2003 (Carlton, 3711503813, SE)

Story: Sidney Fiddler (Sid James) organises a beauty contest in the seaside town of Fircombe – against the wishes of puritanical busybody Augusta Prodworthy (June Whitfield)…

Notable Lines: Kenneth Connor: 'I do believe that Councillor Fiddler has a point there, considering our very high seasonal rainfall figure.' June Whitfield: 'Oh really, Mr Mayor? Personally I think it is quite an average one.' Sid James: 'If you think nine inches is an average one, you've been spoilt!' / Jack Douglas: 'Mrs Philpotts said to tell you… er… no, I must get this right.' Sid James: 'It's all right – I've got all night.' Jack Douglas: 'Er no, that wasn't it.' / Joan Sims: 'You and a bunch of beauty queens? It's like asking Dracula to look after a blood bank!' / Barbara Windsor: 'She's got one bigger than the other.' Sid James: 'Is that right?' Barbara Windsor: 'No – left.' / June Whitfield: 'We will squat in this erection to man's so-called superiority.' / Sid James: 'All the contestants you will see here today represent the very cream of their profession. And cream, let me tell you, that comes in the most magnificent containers. Ah ha ha!'

Observations: For some bizarre reason, June Whitfield dubs all Valerie Leon's lines. When Jimmy Logan first visits the hotel he is wearing his glasses in long shot but not in close-up (and in this scene he also forgets that his character has a lisp). Barbara Windsor clearly looks terrified in the final shot – the reason being that she couldn't ride a motorbike – her bike scenes are mostly done by stuntman Nick Hobbs. The 'Larry' title captions are as follows: Miss Conduct, Miss Conception, Miss Hap, Miss Fortune, Miss Used, Miss Shaped, Miss Trust, Miss Handled, Miss Manage, Miss Placed, Miss Spent, Miss Stake, Miss

Demeanour and Miss Adventure (you can imagine the cartoons!). A Norman Wisdom film called *Press for Time* (1966) also concerned a seaside beauty contest, and coincidentally starred *Girls* actor David Lodge.

All Dragged Up: Bernard Bresslaw as a beauty contestant.

Locations: Brighton, East Sussex, and Slough, Berks.

Review: I love this film, I really do. I know it's much maligned as one of the low points of the *Carry On* series, but I feel it's the closest the gang ever got to typical, allout English seaside postcard humour, as touched on in *Convenience*. It's got great characters, some wonderfully structured farce sequences (Joe Orton, eat your heart out) and the cast are obviously having a whale of a time.

To set the tone, the film opens with a miserable family sheltering from the rain, a sign above them reading, 'Come to Fabulous Fircombe', with underneath a scrawled 'What the hell for?'. There then follows a well-observed council meeting (with Arnold Ridley asleep, reprising his *Dad's Army* role), during which June Whitfield unveils her uncanny impersonation of moral crusader Mary Whitehouse. The look, the voice, the hair – it's all perfect. Kenneth Connor here makes his first appearance as the decrepit Mayor, a performance he would repeat in the next film, *Dick*. Then we cut to the Palace Hotel, a seaside establishment that's run by a domineering harridan (Joan Sims), with a clumsy, incoherent porter (Jack Douglas), a retired major (Peter Butterworth) and a barmy old lady (Joan Hickson). Sounds familiar? Yes, two years before the classic sitcom *Fawlty Towers* aired, we have a perfect prototype, courtesy of the *Carry On* team. (In fact, John Cleese had written a pilot episode as part of the 1971 *Doctor at Large* television series, so it's possible that Peter Rogers and Gerald Thomas had been influenced by that.)

The excellent cast means that Kenneth Williams' absence is hardly noticed. The wonderful Patsy Rowlands is the constantly ill wife of Mayor Kenneth Connor, Sid James is back to being the dodgy wheeler-dealer of *Hancock* days, the outstanding Margaret Nolan raises the blood pressure and even Bernard Bresslaw displays a good grasp of comedy timing. And try as we might, let's not forget the diminutive bike-riding Barbara Windsor, outclassed in the looks department by every other beauty contestant apart from Wendy Richard. The scene where she gets her revenge on lecherous old Peter Butterworth in the lift is marvellous – a small blow for feminism. Speaking of which, Patricia Franklin dresses as a man (the series' only allusion to lesbianism), there's a joke about women not being able to pee standing up (anyone seen *The Full Monty*?) and the whole sequence of the sabotaged beauty parade is a wicked satire on the 1970 Miss World Contest, in which flour bombs and tomatoes were pelted at host Bob Hope by angry feminists (he famously accused them of being 'on dope'). The itching powder gag is resurrected from *Teacher* and the film ends with an exhilarating chase down the pier with Sid on a go-kart. Sheer bliss.

Verdict: This is the last good *Carry On* film and I have pleasure in awarding it a richly deserved **5/5**.

26) Carry On Dick (1974)

Cast: Sid James (Dick Turpin/Reverend Flasher), Kenneth Williams (Captain Desmond Fancey), Barbara

Windsor (Harriett), Jack Douglas (Jock Strapp), Hattie
Jacques (Martha Hoggett), Bernard Bresslaw (Sir Roger
Daley), Joan Sims (Madame Desiree), Peter Butterworth
(Tom), Kenneth Connor (Constable), Bill Maynard
(Bodkin), Patsy Rowlands (Mrs Giles), George Moon (Mr
Giles), Margaret Nolan (Lady Daley), John Clive (Isaak the
Tailor), David Lodge (Bullock), Marianne Stone
(Maggie), Patrick Durkin (William), Sam Kelly
(Coachman), Michael Nightingale (Squire), Brian
Osborne (Browning), Anthony Bailey (Rider), Jeremy
Connor, Nosher Powell (Footpads), Joy Harrington
(Lady), Larry Taylor, Billy Cornelius (Tough Men), Brian
Coburn, Max Faulkner (Highwaymen), Laraine
Humphrys, Linda Hooks, Penny Irving, Eva Reuber-
Staier (Birds of Paradise)

Crew: Director Gerald Thomas, Screenplay Talbot
Rothwell (based on a treatment by Laurie Wyman &
George Evans), Producer Peter Rogers, Music Eric
Rogers, Director of Photography Ernest Steward, Editor
Alfred Roome, Art Director Lionel Couch, Assistant
Editor Jack Gardner, Assistant Director David Bracknell,
Production Manager Roy Goddard, Camera Operator
Jimmy Devis, Continuity Jane Buck, Make-Up Geoffrey
Rodway, Hairdresser Stella Rivers, Costume Designer
Courtenay Elliott, Sound Recordists Danny Daniel &
Ken Barker, Dubbing Editor Peter Best, Set Dresser
Charles Bishop, Casting Director John Owen, Master of
Horse Gerry Wain, Stills Cameraman Tom Cadman,
Wardrobe Mistresses Vi Murray & Maggie Lewis, Coach
& Horses George Mossman (Rank, July 1974,
Eastmancolor, 91m, A/PG)

DVD: 2003 (Carlton, 3711503403, SE)

Story: Captain Fancey (Kenneth Williams) is on the trail of highwayman Dick Turpin (Sid James), but with Captain Jock Strapp (Jack Douglas) to help him it's harder than he first thought...

Notable Lines: Sid James: 'Would you please start playing the wedding music.' Hattie Jacques: 'Very well, Rector – the usual march?' Sid James: 'Fight the Good Fight!' / Barbara Windsor: 'I'd do anything for you, you know that.' Sid James: 'Anything?' Barbara Windsor: 'Anything.' Sid James: 'Well, in that case...' Barbara Windsor: 'Yes?' Sid James: 'Go and... pump the organ.' / Kenneth Williams: 'My dear fellow, they don't call you Jock Strapp for nothing – you don't hang about!' / Sid James: 'I will pray for success to follow up your every endeavour.' Kenneth Williams: 'And up yours too, Rector.' / Kenneth Williams: 'That's not a blasted oak, it's a bloody yew.' / Jack Douglas: 'Pistol!' Kenneth Williams: 'What? I haven't had a drop!' / Hattie Jacques: 'Her husband treats her shamefully, I hear. You'd never believe he was once a Knight.' Sid James: 'It's too much for a woman that age.' / Kenneth Williams: 'Where can we find Dick?' Barbara Windsor: 'Ooh, search me. I've been living here for ten years and I haven't found any.' / Kenneth Connor: 'I'm a silly old constable!'

Key Scene: Nymphomaniac Barbara Windsor tries to seduce the semi-reluctant Sid James who is pretending to chastise her, knowing that Hattie Jacques has her ear to the door.

Observations: The Birds of Paradise manage elaborate costume changes in a matter of seconds. The view out of the open bedroom door of the Cock Inn shows the studio floor beyond, instead of the downstairs drinking hall. The narrator goes uncredited.

All Dragged Up: Sid James and Peter Butterworth as aging tarts.

Locations: Woods and countryside, Iver Heath, Bucks; Hitcham, Bucks.

Review: *Carry On Dick* is a complete waste of everyone's time, especially the viewers'. Everyone's looking like death warmed up, especially Sid James, who turns in a muted performance that contains none of his usual charisma. Kenneth Williams pulls faces in the laziest way imaginable, Hattie Jacques is obviously tired of the whole thing, Kenneth Connor and Patsy Rowlands both look like they've seen better days and Bernard Bresslaw is back to showing how little he knows about playing comedy. Barbara Windsor, continuing a trend that began back in *Henry*, plays the whole thing like she's the principal boy in a matinee of *Cinderella* at Scarborough Civic Centre. I'm very amused that she flashes her breasts and wears a see-through vest in this film, yet turned down *Emmannuelle* because it was too lewd! Jack Douglas is the only cast member to come out of the film with any dignity left intact – despite the fact that the urinal scene is a new low for the series. As for the production, it is depressingly cheap, with underlit, echoey location interiors mixed with underlit, bare Pinewood sets (how bizarre to credit a set dresser), with the occasional bit of grim location filming to provide a semblance of variety.

Dick is the sort of film in which you keep waiting for something vaguely interesting or funny to happen, but it never does. The boring final scenes with Sid James trapped

in the church go on forever and then suddenly it's all over.
I'll leave the last words to Kenneth Williams: 'Wednesday,
20 March 1974... Gerald (Thomas) was saying "Hurry
up, or we'll lose the sun!" and when I quoted some poetry
from Gray to him, he said "We're not here to shoot
poetry! We're here to shoot a load of shit."'

Verdict: Gerald Thomas was quite right. **1/5** (and I'm
being generous).

27) Carry On Behind (1975)

Cast: Kenneth Williams (Professor Roland Crump), Elke
Sommer (Professor Anna Vooshka), Windsor Davies (Fred
Ramsden), Jack Douglas (Ernie Bragg), Bernard Bresslaw
(Arthur Upmore), Patsy Rowlands (Linda Upmore),
Kenneth Connor (Major Leep), Joan Sims (Daphne
Barnes), Peter Butterworth (Henry Barnes), Carol
Hawkins (Sandra), Sherrie Hewson (Carol), Liz Fraser
(Sylvia Ramsden), Ian Lavender (Joe Baxter), Adrienne
Posta (Norma Baxter), Patricia Franklin (Vera Bragg),
Marianne Stone (Mrs Rowan), George Layton (Doctor),
David Lodge (Landlord), Brian Osborne (Bob), Larry
Dann (Clive), Georgina Moon (Sally), Diana Darvey
(Maureen), Jenny Cox (Veronica the Stripper), Larry
Martyn (Electrician), Linda Hooks (Nurse), Billy
Cornelius (Man with Salad), Melita Manger (Woman
with Salad), Ray Edwards (Man with Water), Sidney
Johnson (Man with Glasses), Jeremy Connor (Student
with Ice-Cream), Lucy Griffiths (Woman with Hat),
Alexandra Dane (Woman with Bristols), Hugh Futcher
(Painter), Helli Louise (Nudist), Sam Kelly (Projectionist),
Johnny Briggs (Plasterer), Stanley McGeagh (Short-
Sighted Man), Brenda Cowling (Wife), Drina Pavlovic

(Courting Girl), Caroline Whitaker (Student), Kenneth Waller (Barman)

Crew: Director Gerald Thomas, Screenplay Dave Freeman, Producer Peter Rogers, Music Eric Rogers, Director of Photography Ernest Steward, Editor Alfred Roome, Art Director Lionel Couch, Assistant Editor Jack Gardner, Assistant Director David Bracknell, Production Manager Roy Goddard, Camera Operator Neil Binney, Continuity Marjorie Lavelly, Make-Up Geoffrey Rodway, Hairdresser Stella Rivers, Costume Designer Courtenay Elliott, Sound Recordists Danny Daniel & Ken Barker, Dubbing Editor Pat Foster, Set Dresser Charles Bishop, Caravans supplied by CI Caravans Ltd (Rank, December 1975, Eastmancolor, 90m, A/PG)

DVD: 2003 (Carlton, 3711503473, SE)

Story: University Professors Roland Crump (Kenneth Williams) and Anna Vooshka (Elke Sommer) join forces on an archaeological dig adjacent to a campsite...

Notable Lines: Windsor Davies: 'Me ball's burning!' Peter Butterworth: 'Don't stand so close to the fire.' / Elke Sommer: 'Hello, how are your doings?' / Elke Sommer: 'Perhaps you're finding something in the alluvial.' Peter Butterworth: 'Don't tell me it's blocked up again.' / Elke Sommer (referring to Kenneth Williams): 'Is Professor of Archaeology. Is bleeding terrible.' Windsor Davies: 'Never mind his qualifications – is he hurt badly?' / Kenneth Williams: 'Me theodolite's broken!' Jack Douglas: 'What'll we do!' Windsor Davies: 'We'd better put a splint on that too!' / Kenneth Connor: 'Only a damn swine would try and get a girl drunk first.' Joan Sims: 'First?' Kenneth

Connor: 'It would be a damn waste of time getting her drunk afterwards.'

Key Scene: There's a very touching scene between Peter Butterworth and Joan Sims as the once-married couple reunited after ten years. They both play it straight and, in the midst of all the substandard humour on display elsewhere, these two veterans of the series steal the show.

Observations: The electrician (Larry Martyn) in the major's office disappears between shots. In a rare bid for realism, the action is set during the Easter holiday (at the actual time the film was made), yet the girls go round in skimpy bikinis.

Locations: Maidenhead Town Hall, Berks; Pinewood Green and Pinewood Studios' orchard, Pinewood, Bucks; Farnham Common, Bucks.

Review: Don't be fooled by the name – this is merely a remake of *Carry On Camping*, minus any subtlety the original might have had. The title refers either to Kenneth Williams' 'Getting to the Bottom Of It' lecture or the incident involving wet paint and trouser seats; or perhaps it's just there to justify an animated title sequence of various wiggling posteriors (accompanied by an irritatingly catchy theme tune of the Chas 'n' Dave variety – I challenge you not to hum it long after the film is over). Whatever the reason, most of my comments about *Camping* apply here – the plotlessness, the lack of character interaction etc. – but this time you also get more sex (such as the topless stripper at the start, the long strip scene at the end and the explicit Roman mosaic of a woman holding a bloke's wedding tackle – a bit strong for a PG certificate!). Borrowing an idea from *Convenience* we have a wife with a (foul-beaked) mynah bird, and together with a large dog that causes mischief, it's a further sign that new scriptwriter Dave Freeman was replacing innuendo with slapstick (such as Elke Sommer's speeded-up car crash). The film is just a series of unfunny sketches, minus punchlines, accompanied by too much silly music – a sure sign of a weak script.

Jack Douglas and Windsor Davies are the main double act, and while the former is watchable enough, Davies' rigid performance is far more suited to his role as a soldier in the next film, *England*. Ian Lavender appears, presumably on the strength of his *Dad's Army* role, but is given nothing to do. Unexpectedly, the best performance comes from Kenneth Connor as the randy old Major who gets turned on by brass band music. Patsy Rowlands is given a standard fishwife part and Kenneth Williams appears to be mugging on autopilot. Elke Sommer, though, is surprisingly good as the funny-speaking foreigner who keeps getting her words muddled up ('arse' instead of 'hearts' is one of the more hilarious examples). But it takes more than a few odd gems to turn this into anything other than dross. As Kenneth Williams wrote in his *Diaries* of 22 January 1975, 'Read the *Carry On Behind* script. It is the *worst* I've ever read.' I believe this is a correct summation of the case, M'lud.

Verdict: 'Oh, stop messin' about!' is Williams' totally out-of-character final line, as if this blast from the past will redeem everything. It won't. **1/5**.

28) Carry On England (1976)

Cast: Kenneth Connor (Captain S Melly), Windsor Davies (Sergeant Major 'Tiger' Bloomer), Jack Douglas

(Bombardier Ready), Judy Gleeson (Sergeant Tilly Willing), Peter Jones (Brigadier), Melvyn Hayes (Gunner Shorthouse), Peter Butterworth (Major Carstairs), Joan Sims (Private Jennifer Ffoukes-Sharpe), Diana Langton (Private Alice Easy), Julian Holloway (Major Butcher), David Lodge (Captain Bull), Larry Dann (Gunner Shaw), Brian Osborne (Gunner Owen), Patricia Franklin (Corporal Cook), Johnny Briggs (Melly's Driver), Linda Hooks (Nurse), Vivienne Johnson (Freda), John Carlin, Michael Nightingale (Officers), Jeremy Connor (Gunner Hiscocks), Richard Olley (Gunner Parker), Peter Banks (Gunner Thomas), Billy J Mitchell (Gunner Childs), Richard Bartlett (Gunner Drury), Peter Quince (Gunner Sharpe), Paul Toothill (Gunner Gale), Tricia Newby (Private Murray), Louise Burton (Private Evans), Jeannie Collings (Private Edwards), Barbara Hampshire (Private Carter), Linda Regan (Private Taylor), Barbara Rosenblat (ATS)

Crew: Director Gerald Thomas, Screenplay David Pursall & Jack Seddon, Producer Peter Rogers, Music Max Harris, Director of Photography Ernest Steward, Editor Richard Marden, Art Director Lionel Couch, Assistant Editor Jack Gardner, Assistant Director Jack Causey, Production Manager Roy Goddard, Camera Operator Godfrey Godar, Continuity Marjorie Lavelly, Make-Up Geoffrey Rodway, Hairdresser Stella Rivers, Costume Designer Courtenay Elliott, Sound Recordists Danny Daniel & Gordon McCallum, Dubbing Editor Pat Foster, Set Dresser Donald Picton, Casting Director John Owen, Wardrobe Vi Murray & Don Mothersil, Stills Cameraman Ken Bray, Gun provided by the Imperial War Museum (Rank, October 1976, Eastmancolor, 89m, A/PG)

DVD: 2003 (Carlton, 3711503483, SE)

Story: In 1940, Captain Melly (Kenneth Connor) is given a challenging task – to turn the 1313 Experimental Battery into a fighting force…

Notable Lines: Windsor Davies: 'Do your flies up, that man – your brains is catching cold!' / Kenneth Connor: 'Are you a ventriloquist?' Jack Douglas: 'No, sir – Church of England.' / Kenneth Connor (to his Great Dane): 'Heel, Hitler!' / Kenneth Connor: 'Sergeant Major, when I said that's all, I didn't mean that's all – I meant that's all, that's all.' Windsor Davies: 'Sounds like a lot of alls to me sir.'

Key Scene: During Kenneth Connor's first inspection of the troops, Larry Dann dons a false moustache and impersonates him, complete with manic blinking. Connor starts blinking too ('I'm not blinking, you are!'). This comic impasse is broken only by Windsor Davies who sticks his head in-between them and out-stares them both.

Observations: The bra that Patrick Mower holds disappears between shots. The topless parade scene was heavily trimmed in order to get an 'A' certificate (although the DVD has the uncut version). The 'knickers on the flag-pole' joke was lifted from *Follow That Camel*.

All Dragged Up: Kenneth Connor as a moustachioed ATS.

Location: Pinewood administration building.

Review: More extended sitcom episode (think *Dad's Army* crossed with *Get Some In!*) than proper film, this is a curiously old-fashioned throwback to *Carry On Sergeant,* which, despite its dull location and lack of prime *Carry On* stars, is slightly better than it should be. Perhaps it's Kenneth Connor's rock-solid performance as the blustering Captain Melly (with shades of Charlie Chaplin's waddling gait) that gives this film an edge over its predecessor. Partnered with Windsor Davies (who brings his no-nonsense Battery Sergeant Major character from BBC sitcom *It Ain't Half Hot Mum* (1974–81) to the big screen to great effect), they provide the only reason for watching *England*; the other performances are universally dreadful. Whoever thought Patrick Mower and Judy Gleeson could do comedy should be fired. From a cannon. Joan Sims is treated very badly with an inconsequential role, Peters Jones and Butterworth try their best with a horrible series of 'so bad they're bad' jokes and Diana Langton impresses solely by sticking her chest out like Barbara Windsor.

There are many terrible sequences. Kenneth Connor pretending to be a Nazi plane is probably the nadir of the series. But don't forget the pathetic scenes of scrabbling up and down tunnels from one hut to another that provide one of the series' most blatant pieces of padding, or the exploitative shot of the girls waking up topless (far worse than the infamous topless parade – at least *that* was the punchline to a joke, rather than titillation for its own sake), or Kenneth Connor visiting the toilet after he swallows a button… there are plenty more, but I get depressed when I think about them. Add to all this the cheap look of the production, the dire use of stock footage in the 'climax', the sombre title sequence with its downbeat music, and you wonder just what Peter Rogers and Gerald Thomas thought they were doing.

Verdict: If only to see the double act of Kenneth Connor and Windsor Davies, I give this **2/5**.

29) That's Carry On (1978)

Cast: Everyone

Crew (for new sequences only): Director Gerald Thomas, Screenplay Tony Church, Producer Peter Rogers, Music Eric Rogers, Director of Photography Toni Imi, Editor Jack Gardner, Production Manager Roy Goddard, Sound Recordists Danny Daniel & Ken Barker, Sound Editor Christopher Lancaster (Rank/EMI, February 1978, 95m, A/PG)

DVD: 2003 (Carlton, 3711503833, SE)

Story: Kenneth Williams and Barbara Windsor invade an empty cinema and show clips from old *Carry On* films.

Oddity: *Carry On England* is missing from the line-up, despite being part of the accurate statistic of 28 films mentioned. Presumably because it's crap.

Key New Scene: Not much to choose from here, but Kenneth Williams' masterful tirade against modernity behind the closing credits is a great bit of oratory, bringing back memories of his corpse-inducing Churchillian speech in *Cleo*.

Location: Projection Room 7, Pinewood Studios.

Review: I detest film and television compilations. To cut up carefully structured stories and use bits and pieces of them to make another product smacks of desperation. So it'll be no surprise to discover that I don't much like *That's Carry On*. The title caption appears over a shot of a dog peeing against a wall (from *Carry On Girls*) and that just about sums up my feelings about this whole sorry farrago. A string of clips (some good, some bad) are desultorily dropped into a cheaply shot linking sequence with two stars who are clearly enjoying themselves far more than the audience. Films are presented in roughly chronological order, although often ruined by bad editing (notably, *Follow That Camel*). Stick to watching the proper films – even the bad ones are infinitely more enjoyable than this mess.

Verdict: As a TV filler it might be almost passable, but as a cinema offering it beggars belief. **0/5**.

30) Carry On Emmannuelle (1978)

Cast: Kenneth Williams (Emile Prévert), Suzanne Danielle (Emmannuelle Prévert), Jack Douglas (Lyons), Kenneth Connor (Leyland), Joan Sims (Mrs Dangle), Peter Butterworth (Richmond), Larry Dann (Theodore Valentine), Beryl Reid (Mrs Valentine), Albert Moses (Doctor), Tricia Newby (Surgery Nurse), Howard Nelson (Harry Hernia), Henry McGee (Harold Hump), Claire Davenport (Pub Blonde), Tim Brinton (BBC Newscaster), Corbett Woodall (ITN Newscaster), Eric Barker (General), Robert Dorning (Prime Minister), Bruce Boa (US Ambassador), David Hart (Customs Officer), Dino Shaffek (Emigration Officer), Victor Maddern (Man in Laundrette), Norman Mitchell (Drunken Sailor), Jack Lynn (Admiral of the Fleet), Michael Nightingale (Police Commissioner), Llewellyn

Rees (Lord Chief Justice), Steve Plytas (Arabian Official), Joan Benham (Cynical Lady), Marianne Maskell (Hospital Nurse), Louise Burton (Girl at Zoo), Gertan Klauber (German Soldier), Malcolm Johns (Sentry), John Carlin (French Parson)

Crew: Director Gerald Thomas, Screenplay Lance Peters, Producer Peter Rogers, Music Eric Rogers ('Love Crazy' by Kenny Lynch, sung by Masterplan), Director of Photography Alan Hume, Editor Peter Boita, Art Director Jack Shampan, Assistant Editor Jack Gardner, Assistant Director Gregory Dark, Assistant Production/Unit Manager Roy Goddard, Production Executive for Cleves Investment Ltd Donald Langdon, Camera Operator Godfrey Godar, Continuity Marjorie Lavelly, Make-Up Robin Grantham, Hairdresser Betty Sherriff, Costume Designer Courtenay Elliott, Sound Recordists Danny Daniel & Otto Snel, Dubbing Editor Peter Best, Set Dresser John Hoesli, Wardrobe Margaret Lewin, Stills Cameraman Ken Bray (Hemdale, November 1978, Technicolor, 88m, AA/15)

DVD: 2003 (Carlton, 3711503493, SE)

Story: The French Ambassador (Kenneth Williams) tries to control his nymphomaniac wife (Suzanne Danielle), but to no avail...

Notable Lines: Dino Shaffek: 'What is your husband's occupation?' Suzanne Danielle: 'I am.' / Kenneth Williams: 'She has been travelling all around the world – and other places!' / Joan Sims: 'They're having a phonographic orgy!' / Kenneth Williams: 'I am completely bent!' / Beryl Reid: 'He's a very clever doctor, Dr Jones. If you were at death's door, he'd pull you through.' Larry Dann: 'That's what I'm afraid of.' / Kenneth Connor: 'I'm driving you now, you know, in a Daimler Pervertable – the hood doesn't go down, but the chauffeur does.' / Kenneth Connor: 'You for coffee?' Peter Butterworth: 'No thanks, I'm staying here.' / Kenneth Williams: 'Oh, I've come over all queer!'

Key Scene: The most impressive section of the film is where Kenneth Connor, Jack Douglas, Joan Sims and Peter Butterworth discuss their amorous encounters. Kenneth Connor's story is stylishly presented in the form of a silent comedy, while Sims and Victor Maddern share a truly hysterical scene in a laundrette, seductively putting their undies in the washing machine to the tune of 'The Stripper'.

Observations: Kenneth Connor provides the voice of Harry Hernia. Beryl Reid accuses Larry Dann of being up to no good in his room, 'like that disgusting boy in the novel'. What novel could this be? *A Clockwork Orange*? *Catcher in the Rye*? We should be told.

Locations: Pinewood Green, Pinewood, Bucks; Wembley, London and Central London.

Review: Received wisdom has it that *Emmannuelle* is the worst of the *Carry On* series – a seedy, soft-porn exploitation flick that is as unfunny as it is tasteless. Well, I've got news for you – received wisdom is wrong. *Emmannuelle* is actually a fairly amusing film, certainly far less explicit than *Behind*, *Girls* or even *England*. Apart from tantalising glimpses of Suzanne Danielle's upper torso, the only pair of breasts visible on screen is courtesy of a quick flash from nurse Tricia Newby. There's no real titillation and the lustful encounters are more coy than coarse. It is rumoured that the filmmakers tried to copy the successful *Confessions* film series, but in that case they had a very long way to go! *Emmannuelle* continues the phallic jokes started way back in *Up the Jungle* (amongst others) with the Concorde nose-cone lifting up and the sword atop the Old Bailey being raised, but this is hardly the stuff of soft porn. They're just juvenile visual gags, as harmless as anything Spike Milligan or the *Monty Python* team ever did. True, there are some borderline jokes ('Steward, are you coming?' asks a passenger, as Suzanne Danielle runs a hand down his thigh), but most of the time it's pretty inoffensive stuff.

As to the cast, Suzanne Danielle gives a very creditable performance in a role finely balanced between raunchiness and humour (although perhaps the fact she's half-naked most of the time is influencing my judgment here). Kenneth Williams struts about doing a poncey French accent, while Jack Douglas is curiously muted as the Butler 'Loins'. Peter Butterworth is charming as the white-haired old retainer, Joan Sims issues a quiet air of authority and Kenneth Connor – looking less grizzled than in recent film appearances – does a convincing dirty old man. Larry Dann seems superfluous to the mix, but Beryl Reid as his mother gives a smashing performance, surprisingly her only appearance in a *Carry On* film.

The extensive London location filming has a fresh, breezy feel to it – a world away from the grubby, cut-price air of *Dick* or *England* – and the production itself is generally fine. At the end of the day, it's not very funny or very sexy, so I can understand why it failed to appeal to the punters used to the soft porn of *Confessions* or the glory days of old *Carry Ons*, but I think it's not the nadir that people often make it out to be. I laughed a few times, and that's more than can be said for many of the later entries in the series. Kenneth Williams' *Diaries* comment of the 26 April 1978 is quite apposite: 'I'm amazed at Gerald (Thomas) passing some of the otiose dialogue we have to contend with. I keep thinking "It wasn't as bad as this in the old days" & then I think again and admit "Oh yes it was!"'

Verdict: Not the best, but certainly not the worst, I give this **3/5**.

31) Carry On Columbus (1992)

Cast: Jim Dale (Christopher Columbus), Peter Richardson (Bert Columbus), Bernard Cribbins (Mordecai Mendoza), Sara Crowe (Fatima), Maureen Lipman (Countess Esmeralda), Alexei Sayle (Achmed), Rik Mayall (Sultan), Nigel Planer (Wazir), Julian Clary (Don Juan Diego), Keith Allen (Pepi the Poisoner), Leslie Phillips (King Ferdinand), June Whitfield (Queen Isabella), Richard Wilson (Don Juan Felipe), Rebecca Lacey (Chiquita), Jon Pertwee (Duke of Costa Brava), Jack Douglas (Marco the Cereal Killer), Burt Kwouk (Wang), Andrew Bailey (Genghis), Philip Herbert (Ginger), Martin Clunes (Martin), Tony Slattery (Baba), David Boyce (Customer without Ear), Sara Stockbridge (Nina the Model), Holly Aird (Maria), James Faulkner (Torquemada), Don MacLean (Inquisitor with Ham Sandwiches), Dave Freeman, Duncan Duff, Jonathan Tafler, James Pertwee, Toby Dale, Michael Hobbs (Inquisitors), Peter Grant (Cardinal), Peter Gilmore (Governor of the Canaries), Su Douglas (Countess Joanna), John Antrobus (Manservant), Lynda Baron (Meg),

Allan Corduner (Sam), Nejdet Salih (Fayid), Mark Arden (Mark), Silvestre Tobias (Abdullah), Danny Peacock (Tonto the Torch), Don Henderson (Bosun), Harold Berens (Cecil the Torturer), Marc Sinden (Captain Perez), Charles Fleischer (Pontiac), Larry Miller (Chief), Chris Langham (Hubba), Reed Martin (Poca Hontas), Prudence Solomon (Ha Ha), Peter Gordeno (Shaman)

Crew: Director Gerald Thomas, Screenplay Dave Freeman (additional material by John Antrobus), Producer John Goldstone, Music John du Prez ('Carry On Columbus' written and produced by Malcolm McLaren & Lee Gorman, performed by Jayne Collins & Debbie Holmes), Director of Photography Alan Hume, Editor Chris Blunden, Art Director Peter Childs, Assistant Editor Steve Maguire, Assistant Directors Gareth Tandy, Terry Bamber & Becky Harris, Assistant Art Director Edward Ambrose, Production Supervisor Joyce Herlihy, Executive Producer Peter Rogers, Camera Operator Martin Hume, Make-Up Sarah Monzani & Amanda Knight, Hairdresser Sue Love & Sarah Love, Wardrobe Ken Crouch, Sue Honeyborne, Jane Lewis & Jo Korer, Sound Recordist Chris Munro, Chief Dubbing Editor Otto Snel, Set Decorator Denise Exshaw, Casting Director Jane Arnell (Island World, October 1992, Colour, 91m, PG)

DVD: 2004, Region 1 (Jef Films, B00064AMAS)

Story: Chris Columbus (Jim Dale) and his brother Bert (Peter Richardson) embark on a perilous voyage to discover the Americas. Unfortunately, they find it…

Notable Lines: Rik Mayall: 'And what is the street value of this pepper? Come on, own up!' Bert Kwouk: 'I know nothing. In China we have no streets.' / Julian Clary: 'This is Marco, the serial killer.' Jim Dale: 'Serial killer?' Julian Clary: 'Beats his victims to death with a sack of Rice Krispies.' / Julian Clary: 'I tell you what – you have this end, I'll have the other, and if you get lonely you can always come up my end.' / Bernard Cribbins: 'It's not easy navigating in Hebrew. If I'm not careful, we'll be sailing backwards.' / Rebecca Lacey: 'Hello Marco, what are you looking at?' Jack Douglas: 'Sharks. Man-eating sharks. This sea's full of them. Eh, you mind you don't fall in.' Rebecca Lacey: 'Oh my goodness. You don't think they'd eat me whole?' Jack Douglas: 'No, I'm told they spit that out.' / Maureen Lipman: 'Could you ask your friend to row us ashore?' Rebecca Lacey: 'He will if he can find some oars.' Maureen Lipman: 'What he does when he gets there is his concern.'

Key Scene: The bit where the Shaman makes rain fall on Jim Dale's head... sorry, but I like it.

Observations: September 11 is mooted as the date upon which strange events happen.

All Dragged Up: Sara Crowe as Alexei Sayle's nephew, Tima.

Location: Frensham Ponds, Surrey.

Review: A new *Carry On* film after 14 years was bound to fail. If the producers had roped in all the surviving members, they'd be accused of staleness; if they'd got in a fresh young cast with a 1990s sense of humour, the traditionalists would be up in arms. So they did the only thing they could – they tried both styles, and failed. *Columbus,* at best, is a weak pastiche of the later films. At worst, it is a horribly dull and unfunny mess. The cast itself is extraordinary – the most comedians ever assembled for a British film, bar none. The trouble is, hardly any of these talented performers are allowed anywhere near a joke. Blink and you'll miss Tony Slattery, Rik Mayall and Nigel Planer. They should have got a reasonable slice of the action, but no, after the first scene they don't reappear. And the old team don't fare much better either. June Whitfield, Leslie Phillips and Jon Pertwee barely make an appearance, while poor old Jack Douglas is only given one scene of any note (although it is a *very* funny scene). Instead, we have Bernard Cribbins (bland), Peter Richardson (blander still), Julian Clary (excellent) and Jim Dale (long in the tooth, and as funny as ever, i.e. not much) as the main foursome, with the promising Sara Crowe as token female. Many other actors such as Keith Allen, Richard Wilson and John Antrobus try their hardest, but against the all-consuming naffness of the product, it's an uphill battle. The American contingent, Charles Fleischer and Larry Miller, although amusing to a degree, seem to be acting in a completely different film.

Columbus is neither all-out satire, nor full-blown spoof; it's too boring for a kid's film, too lightweight for an adult comedy. It can never make up its mind what it wants to be, and the finished result is a film that lacks integrity, cohesion and, most of all, humour. Gerald Thomas directs as if he's ashamed of the material (as well he should be), never letting the audience bond with anyone or get involved in the story – surely a key requirement for any comedy film, from *Helzappopin* to *Planes, Trains and Automobiles*. A good example is the Spanish Inquisition – even to attempt to milk comedy from such an unpromising source, you've got to be totally outrageous, as in Mel Brooks' 'beyond bad taste' musical number in *History of the World Part 1*. But here all scriptwriter Dave Freeman can offer us is a few unfunny chants and the sight of Don MacLean offering Bernard Cribbins a ham sandwich. Now, if it had been a *Crackerjack* pen ('Crackerjack!'), that *would* have been funny.

The production itself is not all bad. For one thing, the music is very impressive – although perhaps *too* impressive for its subject matter – while the *Santa Maria* set is almost convincing (which is more than can be said for the fake seascape behind it). But controversially, I reckon the best thing about the film is the closing song ('There she blows – Carry On Columbus!'), written by former *Sex Pistols* manager Malcolm McLaren. It's great fun, and if the film itself had been anywhere near this fresh and exciting, it could have been something very special indeed. But it wasn't.

Verdict: This last gasp of *Carry On* humour may have a huge cast of accomplished comedians, but they are let down by a spectacularly feeble and unfunny script, worthy only of 1/5. What a sorry way to end the series.

32) Carry On London

Cast: TBA

Crew: Screenplay Paul Minnett & Brian Leveson, Producer George Pavlou, Executive Producer Peter Rogers

Story: A limousine hire company is taking the stars to the Herberts, the British version of the Oscars ®...

137

Observations: At the time of writing, few details were available about this projected new *Carry On* venture. Despite various casting rumours in the popular press, such as *EastEnders* star Daniella Westbrook's involvement (now curtailed), the production office was quick to stress that no official press release has yet been issued. But producer George Pavlou is keen to see his 'baby' on the big screen, and a spokesperson for Carry On London Ltd claims that pre-production is 'progressing nicely'. The company's hope is that this major British comedy will reinvigorate a somewhat tired genre, while also providing the template for many more *Carry On*s in the future. Fingers crossed...

Unused *Carry On* ideas:

Carry On Smoking (Norman Hudis, 1961) – set in a fire station

Carry On Flying (Norman Hudis, 1962) – about RAF recruits

Carry On Spaceman (Norman Hudis, 1962) – raw recruit astronauts

Carry On Again Nurse (George Layton & Jonathan Lyne, 1979) – X-rated sequel to *Nurse*

Carry On Texas (Dave Freeman & Dick Vosburgh, 1987) – *Dallas* spoof

Carry On Down Under (unknown writer, 1988) – *Neighbours* parody

Carry On Nursing/*Carry On Again Nurse* (Don MacLean, 1988) – tamer sequel to *Nurse*

Stage

For reasons of space, the following list is selective.

1) Carry On London! (1973)

Cast: Sid James, Barbara Windsor, Kenneth Connor, Peter Butterworth, Bernard Bresslaw, Jack Douglas, George Truzzi, Billy Tasker, Trudi Van Doorn, Lynn Rogers

Crew: Comedy Director Bill Roberton, Script Talbot Rothwell, Dave Freeman, Eric Merriman & Ian Grant, Designer Tod Kingman

Premiere: 14 September 1973, Birmingham Hippodrome (then 18 months at the Victoria Palace, London from 4 October 1973)

Observations: A seemingly slapdash mix of rehashed TV and film sketches liberally sprinkled with songs and speciality acts, this show proved a huge success. It also bumped up the box-office receipts of the concurrent films *Carry On Girls* and *Carry On Dick* into the bargain. **4/5**.

2) Carry On Laughing (1976)

Cast: Jack Douglas, Kenneth Connor, Peter Butterworth, Liz Fraser, Anne Aston, Beau Daniels, Danny O'Dea, Barbara Sumner, Linda Hooks

Crew: Director Bill Roberton, Script Sam Cree, Designer Saxon Lucas

Premiere: 16 June 1976, Royal Opera House, Scarborough (until September)

Observations: This imaginatively entitled farce, set in a health farm, opened two months after Sid James' death. Liz Fraser, fresh from her return to the fold in *Carry On Behind*, joined the regular team. **3/5**.

3) Wot A Carry On in Blackpool (1992)

Cast: Barbara Windsor, Bernard Bresslaw, Richard Gauntlett, Andrew Grainger, Jacqueline Dunnley, Rachel Woolrich, Melanie Holloway, Natalie Holtom, Jonathon Blazer, Julian Essex Spurrier

Crew: Director Tudor Davies, Script Barry Cryer & Dick Vosburgh, Designer Gareth Bowen

Premiere: 22 May 1992, North Pier, Blackpool (until 25 October)

Observations: The two surviving members of the original *Carry On* team provided familiar laughs in this seaside review show, performed in the guise of a 1940s repertory theatre company. Although the jokes were by now old and tired, the show was very popular, and it was planned to take it on a tour of the UK, but instead the Blackpool run was extended for three months. A fitting postscript to a much-loved phenomenon. **4/5**.

4) Think No Evil of Us – My Life with Kenneth Williams (1996)

Cast: David Benson

Crew: Director & Script David Benson

Script: 2000 (Hamish Hamilton, 024114034X)

Premiere: 12 August 1996, St John's Church Hall, Edinburgh (UK tour followed from 5 November)

Observations: A stunning one-man show exploring the author's intense fascination with the actor, incorporating impersonations, anecdotes and personal reminiscences, and finishing on Williams' (alleged) suicide. **5/5**.

5) Cleo, Camping, Emmannuelle & Dick (1998)

Cast: Geoffrey Hutchings, Gina Bellman, Jacqueline Defferary, Adam Godley, Kenneth MacDonald, Samantha Spiro

Crew: Director & Script Terry Johnson, Designer William Dudley

Premiere: 10 September 1998, Lyttelton Theatre (National Theatre), London

Script: 1998 (Methuen, 0413735001)

Observations: A funny and moving account of the relationship between Barbara Windsor, Sid James and Kenneth Williams with a cast of excellent actors going beyond mimicry to uncover the real personalities beneath the masks. **5/5**.

Television

All programmes are made in colour unless otherwise stated; timings include commercial breaks. Excluded are programmes about individual actors, *Carry On* documentaries and compilation series.

1) Carry On Christmas (1969)

Cast: Sid James, Terry Scott, Charles Hawtrey, Hattie Jacques, Barbara Windsor, Peter Butterworth, Bernard Bresslaw, Frankie Howerd

Crew: Director Ronnie Baxter, Writer Talbot Rothwell, Producer Peter Eton, Designer Roger Allan, Choir Routine Ralph Tobert, Comedy Consultant Gerald Thomas

Broadcast: 24 December 1969, ITV (Thames), 1hr

Video: 1991 (Cinema Club, as Carry On... Christmas Capers)

Observations: A mickey-take of Charles Dickens' *A Christmas Carol*, this spirited comedy was performed in front of a studio audience, with much ad libbing and wandering from the script on the part of the *Carry On*

team. It was made back to back with *Carry On Up the Jungle*, which accounts for the similarity in cast. The best of the TV *Carry Ons*. **5/5**.

2) Carry On Again Christmas (1970)

Cast: Sid James, Terry Scott, Charles Hawtrey, Barbara Windsor, Kenneth Connor, Bernard Bresslaw, Bob Todd, Wendy Richard

Crew: Director & Producer Alan Tarrant, Writers Dave Freeman & Sid Colin, Executive Producer Peter Eton, Designer Roger Allan, Comedy Consultant Gerald Thomas

Alternatively: 'Carry On Long John' or 'I'm Worried about Jim Hawkins'

Broadcast: 24 December 1970, ITV (Thames, b/w), 1hr

Video: 1991 (Cinema Club, as Carry On... Christmas Capers)

Observations: The cast struggle heroically with an inferior script in a second TV outing, this time a parody of *Treasure Island* with Barbara Windsor cast in panto vein as Jim Hawkins. **4/5**.

3) Carry On Christmas (1972)

Cast: Hattie Jacques, Joan Sims, Barbara Windsor, Kenneth Connor, Peter Butterworth, Jack Douglas, Norman Rossington, Brian Oulton, Billy Cornelius, Valerie Leon, Valerie Stanton

Crew: Director Ronnie Baxter, Writers Talbot Rothwell & Dave Freeman, Producer Gerald Thomas, Executive Producer Peter Rogers, Designer Tony Borer, Costumes Frank Van Raay

Alternatively: 'Carry On Stuffing'

Broadcast: 20 December 1972, ITV (Thames), 1hr

Video: 1992 (Video Club, as Carry On... Christmas Capers)

Observations: After a year's absence, the *Carry On* team – minus its star players – returns with Christmas stories set around an eighteenth-century banquet, replete with Benny Hill-style buxom serving wenches (hello, Valerie Leon). There's some gold amongst the dross, but not much. **3/5**.

4) What a Carry On! (1973)

Cast: Sid James, Barbara Windsor, Kenneth Connor, Peter Butterworth, Bernard Bresslaw, Jack Douglas

Crew: Director & Producer Alan Tarrant, Programme Associate Tony Hawes

Broadcast: 4 October 1973, ITV (ATV), 1hr

Observations: Filmed highlights from the stage premiere of *Carry On London!* are intermixed with cast interviews and film clips, all hosted – for some reason – by *Police 5*'s Shaw Taylor. **3/5**.

5) Carry On Christmas (1973)

Cast: Sid James, Joan Sims, Barbara Windsor, Kenneth Connor, Peter Butterworth, Bernard Bresslaw, Jack Douglas, Julian Holloway, Laraine Humphreys

Crew: Director Ronald Fouracre, Writer Talbot Rothwell, Producer Gerald Thomas, Music Associate Norman Stevens, Executive Producer Peter Rogers, Designer Allan Cameron, Choreographer Terry Gilbert

Broadcast: 24 December 1973, ITV (Thames), 1hr

Video: 1992 (Video Club, as Carry On… Christmas Capers)

Observations: A collection of historical sketches (prehistory, eighteenth century, World War I and Robin Hood) linked by Sid James' department-store Santa. With Talbot at the helm for the last time on TV, it's mostly up to standard. **3/5**.

6) Carry On Laughing (1975)

Cast: See individual episodes

Crew: Director Alan Tarrant, Writers Dave Freeman (1–3, 6–8), Lew Schwarz (5, 9–13), Barry Cryer & Dick Vosburgh (4), Producer Gerald Thomas, Music Richard Tattersall & John Marshall, Executive Producer Peter Rogers, Designers Stanley Mills (1), Ray White (2, 5), Richard Lake (3, 4, 6), Lewis Logan (7, 8), Brian Holgate (9, 10), Anthony Waller (11, 12), Michael Bailey (13), Graphics George Wallder, Animator Len Lewis

NB: Series made by ATV and shown on ITV, with all episodes running at 30 minutes. Titles in parenthesis denote the Special Edition DVD that contains the relevant episode.

1) The Prisoner of Spenda

Cast: Sid James, Barbara Windsor, Peter Butterworth, Joan Sims, Kenneth Connor, Jack Douglas, Diane Langton, David Lodge, Rupert Evans, Ronnie Brody

Broadcast: 4 January 1975 (*Don't Lose Your Head*)

Observations: This spoof of the classic novel has Sid James in two roles, but strong work by the regulars can't disguise a weak script.

2) The Baron Outlook

Cast: Sid James, Barbara Windsor, Joan Sims, Kenneth Connor, Peter Butterworth, Linda Hooks, Diane Langton, David Lodge, John Carlin, John Levene, Brian Osborne, Anthony Trent

Broadcast: 11 January 1975 (*Doctor*)

Observations: Medieval hi-jinks of a fairly feeble kind.

3) The Sobbing Cavalier

Cast: Sid James, Barbara Windsor, Jack Douglas, Joan Sims, Peter Butterworth, David Lodge, Brian Osborne, Bernard Holley

Broadcast: 18 January 1975 (*Up the Khyber*)

Observations: The English Civil War is the unlikely scenario for this slice of *Carry On* comedy, but thanks to strong characterisation and convincing historical detail, this is probably the best of the bunch.

4) Orgy and Bess

Cast: Sid James, Hattie Jacques, Kenneth Connor, Barbara Windsor, Jack Douglas, Victor Maddern, McDonald Hobley, Brian Osborne, John Carlin, Norman Chappell

Broadcast: 25 January 1975 (*Camping*)

Observations: The court of Elizabeth I is the backdrop for this, the last *Carry On* effort to feature Sid James and Hattie Jacques.

5) One in the Eye for Harold

Cast: Jack Douglas, Kenneth Connor, Joan Sims, Diane Langton, David Lodge, Linda Hooks, Norman Chappell, Patsy Smart, Brian Osborne, John Carlin, Paul Jesson, Jerold Wells, Billy Cornelius, Nosher Powell

Broadcast: 1 February 1975 (*Again Doctor*)

Observations: The Battle of Hastings (obviously) with Jack Douglas and Kenneth Connor assuming a double act in the absence of most of the *Carry On* veterans.

6) The Nine Old Cobblers

Cast: Jack Douglas, Kenneth Connor, Barbara Windsor, Joan Sims, David Lodge, Victor Maddern, Patsy Rowlands, John Carlin, Sam Harding

Broadcast: 8 February 1975 (*Up the Jungle*)

Observations: Lord Peter Whimsey becomes Lord Peter Flimsy (a restrained Jack Douglas) in this tale of a sinister bell that tolls when murder is afoot.

7) Under the Round Table

Cast: Kenneth Connor, Joan Sims, Peter Butterworth, Bernard Bresslaw, Jack Douglas, Victor Maddern, Oscar James, Norman Chappell, Valerie Walsh, Billy Cornelius, Desmond McNamara, Brian Capron, Ronnie Brody, Brian Osborne

Broadcast: 26 October 1975 (*Loving*)

Observations: The second series begins with this woefully unfunny King Arthur spoof.

8) The Case of the Screaming Winkles

Cast: Jack Douglas, Kenneth Connor, Joan Sims, Peter Butterworth, Sherrie Hewson, David Lodge, Norman Chappell, Marianne Stone, John Carlin, Melvyn Hayes, Michael Nightingale

Broadcast: 2 November 1975 (*at Your Convenience*)

Observations: The second Lord Peter Flimsy play – this time with a nautical flavour.

9) And in My Lady's Chamber

Cast: Kenneth Connor, Barbara Windsor, Joan Sims, Jack Douglas, Peter Butterworth, Bernard Bresslaw, Sherrie Hewson, Andrew Ray, Carol Hawkins, Vivienne Johnson

Broadcast: 9 November 1975 (*Matron*)

Observations: Bedroom-hopping mickey-take of *Upstairs, Downstairs* in the style of the dire 1976 film *Keep It Up Downstairs*.

10) Short Knight, Long Daze

Cast: Kenneth Connor, Joan Sims, Peter Butterworth, Jack Douglas, Bernard Bresslaw, Susan Skipper, Norman Chappell, Brian Osborne, Desmond McNamara, Billy Cornelius, Brian Capron

Broadcast: 16 November 1975 (*Abroad*)

Observations: Another King Arthur spoof, with – if this is possible – even fewer jokes than before.

11) The Case of the Coughing Parrot

Cast: Jack Douglas, Kenneth Connor, Joan Sims, David Lodge, Sherrie Hewson, Peter Butterworth, Norman Chappell, Brian Osborne, Johnny Briggs, Vivienne Johnson

Broadcast: 23 November 1975 (*Dick*)

Observations: The final play starring Jack Douglas as Lord Peter Flimsy is set in the seedy environs of London's docks.

12) Who Needs Kitchener?

Cast: Kenneth Connor, Barbara Windsor, Jack Douglas, Joan Sims, Bernard Bresslaw, Andrew Ray, Sherrie Hewson, Carol Hawkins, Vivienne Johnson, Brian Osborne

Broadcast: 30 November 1975 (*Behind*)

Observations: More *Upstairs, Downstairs* spoofery, this time with a World War I slant. The BBC sitcom *You Rang M'Lord* (1990–3) did it much better. Which says a lot.

13) Lamp-Posts of the Empire

Cast: Kenneth Connor, Barbara Windsor, Jack Douglas, Bernard Bresslaw, Peter Butterworth, Oscar James, Reuben Martin, Wayne Browne, Norman Chappell, Michael Nightingale, John Carlin

Broadcast: 7 December 1975 (*England*)

Observations: The final entry in the series revisits *Carry On Up the Jungle* territory for a tale of British Colonialism gone mad.

Series DVD: 2004, Region 1 (A&E, B0001XARLI)

Series Observations: If this series had been made five years earlier, it might have been a worthy addition to the *Carry On* oeuvre. Unfortunately by 1975 the films were looking tired and stale, and the TV series merely emphasised the scriptwriters' lack of originality and wit. This combined with the absence of key players Kenneth Williams, Charles Hawtrey and (for the most part) Sid James resulted in a largely disappointing series. **2/5**.

7) Carry On Banging (1989)

Cast: Harry Enfield, Jack Douglas, Barbara Windsor, Kenneth Connor

Crew: Director Geoff Posner, Writer Harry Enfield & Geoffrey Perkins, Producer Geoffrey Perkins, Music David Firman, Executive Producer Denise O'Donoghue, Designer Graeme Story, Costumes Sharon Lewis

Broadcast: 3 November 1989 as part of *Norbert Smith – A Life*, C4 (Hat Trick), 60m

Video: 1991 (Universal, B00008T393, on *Norbert Smith – A Life*)

Observations: For this tribute to fictitious actor Norbert Smith, comedian Harry Enfield brought together three original cast members for a three-minute clip from a *Carry On* film, supposedly made in the 1980s about anti-nuclear protesters. A brief but accurate parody. **4/5**.

8) Cor Blimey! (2000)

Cast: Geoffrey Hutchings, Adam Godley, Samantha Spiro,

CARRY ON FILMS

Chrissie Cotteril, Steve Spiers, Hugh Walters, Derek Howard, David McAlister, Barbara Windsor, Claire Cathcart, Windsor Davies

Crew: Director & Writer Terry Johnson, Producer Margaret Mitchell, Executive Producers Charlie Pattinson, George Faber & Suzan Harrison, Music Barrington Pheloung

Broadcast: 24 April 2000, ITV (Carlton), 2hrs

DVD: 2001, Region 1 (BFS, B00005N5R1)

Observations: A TV adaptation of the hit stage play *Cleo, Camping, Emmannuelle & Dick*, this manages to recreate classic *Carry On* scenes with a cast of actors who uncannily resemble their big-screen counterparts. The bittersweet drama is utterly compelling and when Barbara Windsor replaces Samantha Spiro in the closing scene, the transformation is almost unnoticeable. **5/5**.

Reference Materials

Books

For titles about individual cast members, see Biographies section

Carry On Emmannuelle by Lance Peters, 1977

The Carry On Book by Kenneth Eastaugh, 1978

What a Carry On – The Official Story of the Carry On Films by Sally & Nina Hibbin, 1988

Carry On Doctor, Carry On… Up the Khyber, Carry On Loving, Carry On Henry, Carry On Abroad & Carry On England by Norman Giller, 1996

Carry On Laughing by Adrian Rigelsford, 1996

England Is Mine – Pop Life in Albion from Wilde to Goldie by Michael Bracewell, 1998

The Carry On Companion – 40th Anniversary Special Edition by Robert Ross, 1998

Carry On Uncensored by Morris Bright & Robert Ross, 1999

The Lost Carry Ons by Morris Bright & Robert Ross, 2000

The Carry On Book of Statistics by Kevin Snelgrove, 2003

The Complete A–Z of Everything Carry On by Richard Webber, 2005

The Carry On Story: In Pictures by Robert Ross, 2005

Websites

Carry On Line The best website for all things Carry On: www.carryonline.com

Carry On Signing Autographs from the great and good of the Carry On world: http://members.tripod.com/autograph_heaven/

Kenneth Williams – The Complete and Utter Fabulosa Website: www.stopmessinabout.co.uk

Carry On London – If they ever make this one, all the details will be here: www.carryonlondonfilm.com

Carry On Photographing – Fascinating before and after shots of loads of key locations: http://carryon.moviefever.com

Jim Dale Home Page – News and information on the actor's ongoing work: www.jim-dale.com

Internet Movie Database – Your one-stop site for cast and crew filmographies, locations, reviews and miscellaneous trivia: www.imdb.com

Quiz Answers

1)
1) Barbara Windsor in *That's Carry On*
2) Sid James in *Carry On Cowboy*
3) Bob Monkhouse in *Carry On Sergeant*
4) Eric Barker in *Carry On Spying*
5) Ted Ray in *Carry On Teacher*
6) Sid James in *Carry On Henry*
7) Jack Douglas in *Carry On Dick*
8) Terry Scott in *Carry On Loving*

2)
1) Kenneth Williams in *Carry On Cruising*
2) Kenneth Connor in *Carry On Sergeant*
3) Kenneth Williams in *Carry On Constable*
4) Bernard Cribbins in *Carry On Jack*
5) Kenneth Williams in *Carry On Henry*
6) Kenneth Williams in *Carry On Dick*
7) Kenneth Williams in *Carry On Behind*
8) Peter Butterworth in *Carry On England*
9) Peter Butterworth in *(Carry On) Follow That Camel*

3)
1) *Carry On Cruising*
2) *Carry On Jack*
3) *Carry On Doctor*

4) *Carry On Camping*
5) *(Carry On) Follow That Camel*

4)
1) *Carry On Doctor*
2) *Carry On Emmannuelle*
3) *Carry On Henry*
4) *Carry On Jack*
5) *Carry On Teacher*
6) *Carry On Behind*
7) *Carry On Matron*
8) *Carry On Loving*
9) *Carry On Up the Jungle*
10) *Carry On Nurse*
11) *Carry On Columbus*

Contact the author: If you would like to correspond with Mark Campbell and give him some feedback on this Pocket Essential, you can send an email to mark.campbell10@virgin.net

POCKET ESSENTIALS STOCK TITLES

1903047773	Agatha Christie Mark Campbell	4.99
1903047706	Alan Moore Lance Parkin	3.99
1903047528	Alchemy & Alchemists Sean Martin	3.99
1903047005	Alfred Hitchcock Paul Duncan	4.99
1903047722	American Civil War Phil Davies	3.99
1903047730	American Indian Wars Howard Hughes	3.99
1903047757	Ancient Greece Mike Paine	3.99
1903047714	Ang Lee Ellen Cheshire	3.99
1903047463	Animation Mark Whitehead	4.99
1903047676	Audrey Hepburn Ellen Cheshire	3.99
190304779X	The Beastie Boys Richard Luck	3.99
1904048196	The Beatles Paul Charles	3.99
1903047854	The Beat Generation Jamie Russell	3.99
1903047366	Billy Wilder Glenn Hopp	3.99
1903047919	Bisexuality Angie Bowie	3.99
1903047749	Black Death Sean Martin	3.99
1903047587	Blaxploitation Films Mikel J Koven	3.99
1903047455	Bollywood Ashok Banker	3.99
1903047129	Brian de Palma John Ashbrook	3.99
1903047579	Bruce Lee Simon B Kenny	3.99
1904048978	Bruce Springsteen	4.99
190404803X	Carry On Films Mark Campbell	4.99
1904048048	Classic Radio Comedy Nat Coward	3.99
1903047811	Clint Eastwood Michael Carlson	3.99
190304703X	Coen Brothers Cheshire/Ashbrook	4.99
1903047307	Conspiracy Theories Robin Ramsay	3.99
1904048099	Creative Writing Neil Nixon	3.99
1903047536	The Crusades Mike Paine 3.99 (R/P)	
1903047285	Cyberpunk Andrew M Butler	3.99
1903047269	David Cronenberg John Costello	3.99
1903047064	David Lynch Le Blanc/Odell	3.99
1903047196	Doctor Who Mark Campbell	4.99
1904048277	Do Your Own PR Richard Milton	3.99
190304751X	Feminism Susan Osborne	3.99
1903047633	Film Music Paul Tonks	3.99
1903047080	Film Noir Paul Duncan	3.99
1904048080	Film Studies Andrew M Butler	4.99
190304748X	Filming on a Microbudget NE Paul Hardy	4.99
190304765X	French New Wave Chris Wiegand	4.99
1903047544	Freud & Psychoanalysis Nick Rennison	3.99
1904048218	Georges Simenon David Carter	3.99
1903047943	George Lucas James Clarke	3.99
1904048013	German Expressionist Films Paul Cooke	3.99
1904048161	Globalisation Steven P McGiffen	3.99
1904048145	Hal Hartley Jason Wood	3.99
1904048110	Hammer Films John McCarty	3.99
1903047994	History of Witchcraft Lois Martin	3.99
1903047404	Hitchhiker's Guide M J Simpson	4.99
1903047072	Hong Kong's Heroic Bloodshed Martin Fitzgerald 3.99 (R/P)	
1903047382	Horror Films Le Blanc/Odell	3.99
1903047692	Jack the Ripper Whitehead/Rivett	3.99
1903047102	Jackie Chan Le Blanc/Odell	3.99
1903047951	James Cameron Brian J Robb	3.99
1903047242	Jane Campion Ellen Cheshire	3.99
1904048188	Jethro Tull Raymond Benson	3.99
1903047374	John Carpenter Le Blanc/Odell	3.99

1904048285	The Knights Templar Sean Martin 9.99 hb
1903047250	Krzystzof Kieslowski Monika Maurer 3.99 (R/P)
1903047609	Laurel & Hardy Brian J Robb 3.99
1903047803	The Madchester Scene Richard Luck 3.99
1903047315	Marilyn Monroe Paul Donnelley 3.99
1903047668	Martin Scorsese Paul Duncan 4.99
1903047595	The Marx Brothers Mark Bego 3.99
1903047846	Michael Mann Mark Steensland 3.99
1903047641	Mike Hodges Mark Adams 3.99
1903047498	Nietzsche Travis Elborough 3.99 (R/P)
1903047110	Noir Fiction Paul Duncan 3.99
1904048226	Nuclear Paranoia C Newkey-Burden 3.99
1903047927	Oliver Stone Michael Carlson 3.99
1903047048	Orson Welles Martin Fitzgerald 3.99
1904048366	Quentin Tarantino 4.99
1903047293	Philip K Dick Andrew M Butler 3.99
1904048242	Postmodernism Andrew M Butler 3.99
1903047560	Ridley Scott Brian Robb 3.99
1903047838	The Rise of New Labour Robin Ramsay 3.99
1904048102	Roger Corman Mark Whitehead 3.99
1903047897	Roman Polanski Daniel Bird 3.99
1903047447	Science Fiction Films 4.99
1903047412	Sergio Leone Michael Carlson 3.99
1903047684	Sherlock Holmes Mark Campbell 3.99
1903047277	Slasher Movies Mark Whitehead 3.99
1904048072	Spike Lee Darren Arnold 3.99
1903047013	Stanley Kubrick Paul Duncan 3.99
190304782X	Steven Soderbergh Jason Wood 3.99
1903047439	Steven Spielberg James Clarke 4.99
1903047331	Stock Market Essentials Victor Cuadra 3.99
1904048064	Succeed in Music Business Paul Charles 3.99
1903047765	Successful Sports Agent Mel Stein 3.99
1903047145	Terry Gilliam John Ashbrook 3.99
1903047390	Terry Pratchett Andrew M Butler 3.99
1903047625	Tim Burton Le Blanc/Odell 4.99
190404817X	Tintin J M & R Lofficier 3.99
1903047889	UFOs Neil Nixon 3.99
1904048250	The Universe Richard Osborne 9.99 hb
1904048358	Urban Legends 4.99
190304717X	Vampire Films Le Blanc/Odell 3.99
190404820X	Videogaming Flatley & French 3.99
1903047935	Vietnam War Movies Jamie Russell 3.99
1904048129	Who Shot JFK? Robin Ramsay 3.99
1904048056	William Shakespeare Ian Nichols 3.99
1903047056	Woody Allen Martin Fitzgerald 3.99
1903047471	Writing a Screenplay John Costello 4.99